Testimonials

"From surfer dude to star athlete to star veterinarian, Dr. Coward spins a great tale of his life and career caring not only for himself, but also his thousands of amazing patients using a combination of traditional medicine and healthy nutrition. *Healing Both Ends of the Leash* is an intriguing read!"

—Doug Mader, MS, DVM, author of the award-winning book *The Vet at Noah's Ark*

"For an incredible three-year period, Doug taught me more than I can ever say—plus we eagerly shared the path of Whole-istic healing to help animals live joyous, loving and healthy lives. This must-read book shares Dr. Doug's knowledge, wisdom, experiences, and reverence for all life to empower us all to be the best parents possible."

—Gail Pope, founder of BrightHaven Center for Animal Rescue, Hospice and Holistic Education, and cohost of the *Peace of Mind for Pet Parents Podcast*

"*Healing Both Ends of the Leash* is a necessary read in a veterinary culture that processed foods are the status quo. This book instills hope for pet parents to know how to make changes before their animals get sick, during sickness, and in their senior years. One can only give away what one has first practiced. Dr. Coward, through his intentional living, 'Our best protection has always been sleep, sunshine, breath, whole foods, and love,' shows how things we tend to minimize in our culture are healing both to animals and humans. He will inspire you to let nature and food therapy help heal you. The book highlights the importance of healing from the inside out.

A simple yet profound truth that Dr. Coward shares through-out the book illustrated through the many touching stories that will leave you laughing, smiling, crying, and inspired to give your pets the best life possible—and improve your own health too! Dr. Coward is a traveler, adventurer, surfer, hus-band, father, and the most compassionate veterinarian you will ever meet. A true Healer."

—Renee Baffert, MA, grief pet loss counselor, producer and writer of award-winning documentary *Eben*

"Charming and written in an engaging style full of stories about Dr. Doug's life and veterinary clinic experiences with so many of the precious sentient beings we share on this planet."

—W. Jean Dodds, DVM, award-winning author of *Canine Nutrigenomics* and *The Canine Epidemic*

"Doug brings the same passion to writing *Healing Both Ends of the Leash* that he brought to the basketball court at Santa Clara University and then in the Australian basketball league. The stories are entertaining and educational for anyone car-ing for a beloved family pet, a young athlete seeking optimal health, or anyone with chronic disease who has never heard of the healing power of real food. Doug's book is a treasure of health tips for both ends of the leash."

—Carroll Williams, former head basketball coach and athletic director at Santa Clara University

"Dr. Coward has written a transformative book that every pet owner should read. It highlights the profound power and benefits of the right whole foods for our pets' health. His compassion and decades of real-world veterinary experience make him a rare and invaluable resource. If you've found this book, I urge you to embrace its wisdom and apply it to your pet's life."

—Rob Ryan, CEO and cofounder of Gussy's
Gut, The Dog Microbiome Co.

"This is a beautiful book, and it is a pleasure to read such a positive perspective on life. Wouldn't we all love to have a pet vet like Dr. Doug!"

—Dr. Greg and Linda Harrison, coauthors of
Clinical Avian Medicine and Surgery and
founders of Harrison's Bird Foods

HEALING BOTH ENDS OF THE LEASH

Healing Both Ends of the Leash

Doug Coward, DVM

Waterside Productions

First Printing, 2025

ISBN-13: 978-1-968401-24-5 print edition
ISBN-13: 978-1-968401-25-2 ebook edition

Waterside Productions
2055 Oxford Ave
Cardiff, CA 92007
www.waterside.com

For my family: Floy and Ron who gave us our first beloved beagle in 1958.
My brother Dave and sister Nancy who followed the whole food therapy protocol for their family's long-lived golden retrievers and Labs.
Our daughters Kelly and Shawn who have brought such joy, delight, and adventure to our family and who have now blessed us with grandchildren.
My wife Nancy, the world's greatest adventure traveler, who has been there since day one supporting the accidental veterinary journey. Neither this book nor the Animal and Bird Clinic would have ever happened without your kind support and dedicated hard work.
My wonderful parents who tolerated all the lizards and snakes I brought home, and which always escaped their cages. May you rest in peace in the waters off Lanikai.

When diet is wrong, medicine is of no use.
When diet is correct, medicine is of no need.
—Ayurvedic Proverb

"The best remedy for those who are afraid, lonely or unhappy is to go outside, somewhere where they can be quite alone with the heavens, nature and God. Because only then does one feel that all is as it should be and that God wishes to see people happy, amidst the simple beauty of nature."
—Anne Frank

TABLE OF CONTENTS

Part Three: The Animal and Bird Clinic

Part Four: Healing Both Ends of the Leash

FOREWORD

I have watched Dr. Douglas Coward do the impossible since the day he saved the lives of twenty-nine of my hamsters when no one else could.

I study animal behavior, and I had fifty-three hamsters that were all dying of some mysterious disease.

I'd tried every vet I could find who accepted hamsters. But each of them used treatments that were completely ineffective, and twenty-three of my little critters died. By the time I arrived at Dr. Doug's office with the remaining thirty, I was exhausted and devastated.

The first thing I asked him was, "When the next one dies, would you be willing to do a necropsy with culture and sensitivities?" No one else had been willing to, no matter how much money I offered them. It was baffling to me. He readily agreed, and soon another hamster died, leaving me with twenty-nine. Would I lose them all?

To my surprise, I found a handwritten condolence card from him in the mail a few days later, even referring to the deceased hamster by name. I have never seen a vet do that before or since. It turns out that's common practice for him. Lizard, rat, dog, or cat, they all matter equally to him.

By studying the one who had died, he quickly identified that the problem was a rare bacteria, found in wild rabbits, that would only respond to a particular injectable antibiotic, which he immediately provided. Thanks to him, the remaining twenty-nine of my hamsters recovered and lived out their full lives.

Later, he saved the life of my dog, Fiona, a Great Pyrenees mix, who had stopped eating and lost a lot of weight.

He found that her intestines were packed with fur. Any other vet would have treated this with major surgery. But when a dog is already sick and dehydrated, as you can imagine, the outcome of such treatment would typically be death.

Dr. Doug had an entirely different approach.

Fiona was an extremely anxious dog and already struggled with anorexia. So he allowed me to stay in her cage to reassure her while he administered IV fluids for several hours. Then he tube fed her a slippery mix of salmon oil and pureed pumpkin, which saturated the impacted fur so she could pass it naturally and easily.

It wasn't just my animals that were being saved when other vets didn't know what to do. I've seen him bring back to life many people's pets that other vets had said should be euthanized.

He's accumulated wisdom from all over the world while treating elephants and multitudes of other wild creatures.

He reminds me of many of the biologists I have known at Caltech who were like Steve Irwin—living adventurers in pursuit of a greater understanding.

Dr. Doug started out as a professional basketball player and a surfer, but he soon discovered that wild animals were his true passion, and he became a wildlife veterinarian. When he started treating domestic pets, he was surprised at how unhealthy they were compared to animals living in their natural habitat.

He began a relentless search for truth, discovered food therapy, and has been developing groundbreaking therapeutic methods for many decades.

He even met with the Dalai Lama, as he collected wisdom from traditional healers all over the world. He combines Chinese and Ayurvedic medicine with indigenous knowledge of healing plants. And he now employs modern science, along with practical understanding gained over thousands of years, to cure his patients.

His methods are making the lame walk and all but raising the dead.

He directed me to switch my dogs' diet from processed kibble and canned foods to organic meat, fruit, vegetables, and supplements. With his help, they have thrived. I also took his advice on how humans should eat. I lost weight and am on a healing journey from a long illness of my own.

This book is a fascinating account of what he's learned from his individual patients, and his ongoing, passionate quest for understanding.

It puts all his years of gathered knowledge into your hands.

I think you'll find yourself coming back to this resource over and over again.

Dr. Doug's many adventures and discoveries make for an exciting read!

Stacey O'Brien
Author of *Wesley the Owl*

Author's Note

The stories you are about to read are true—some recalled to perfection from over fifty years ago, others hazy recollections of encounters with wildlife, pets, and people. I have boxes of hand-scrawled journals from my youthful adventures in Australia in 1975 and decades of travels to wild places to see wild animals across the globe.

I never planned to be a pet vet for long, so those stories exist only in my memory. I didn't keep a journal about patients, just clinical records for reference. I always envisioned a life spent outdoors with wild animals, and over the years, I made notes of those encounters. Some characters' names have been altered by my fading memory, some by request for anonymity, and many are happy to share their real identities and love for animals.

I once dreamed of writing about a career in the NBA as a professional basketball player or as an intrepid ecologist studying the African savanna or the Amazon rainforest. That never happened. Instead, I became an accidental veterinarian, led down this path by a series of misadventures I was once too embarrassed to share. But everything I thought I knew about veterinary medicine changed the day I met a miracle Labrador at a Central California winery. I knew then that one day, I would tell that story.

Many families began asking if I would write a book about the natural diet and the guidelines we used to help pets heal. They also wondered, often with a mix of curiosity and hope, whether these same principles could help people too. At the time, our veterinary practice was thriving, our young daughters were growing up fast, and I was still learning everything I could about caring for multiple species in a rapidly changing world of medicine and technology. Rather than sit down to write, I chose to greet the sunrise in the surf. This was my daily antidote to what I call nature deficit disorder, or NDD.

Since childhood, I've craved the grounding pulse of the natural world. It's where I've always found my balance. And when my health collapsed a decade ago, I finally turned inward, researching how to heal myself and wondering if the very same holistic practices I recommended for animals could work for humans too. I had no idea how difficult that journey would be, or how deeply it would affirm what I already believed. In hindsight, I probably should have just written about animal healing, which was straightforward, while human healing was so enigmatic, filled with twists and turns beyond my imagination.

Since my earliest dreams weren't of medicine, but of basketball, I was like many young athletes who believed the price of greatness was constant effort and very little sleep. Unfortunately, that belief wrecked my health before I even knew what wellness was. I lived on sugar, rarely drank water, and thought five hours of sleep a night was plenty. Looking back, I wish someone had handed me *Why We Sleep* by Dr. Matthew Walker and told me about the dozens of medical benefits of seven hours of sleep, such as the glymphatic system that detoxifies the brain each night.

But it would take years—and many personal setbacks—before I learned how critical rest, food, water, movement, and connection to nature are for healing and longevity.

These are the stories I share with families to give them hope for healing pets with cancer, arthritis, autoimmune disease, kidney failure, ravaged itchy skin, diabetes, diarrhea, and other chronic illnesses. I don't lecture them on the magnificent biochemistry of mitochondria or the marvels of the intestinal immune system. As my mentor, Doc, always said: *Keep it simple, sweetheart*: the KISS principle.

These stories serve as guidelines for healing pets and people, meant to complement the findings of your veterinarian or medical doctor. To save trees and keep this book affordable, I've listed all the reference books I've read on a Facebook page, **Healing Both Ends of the Leash**, where I'll continue to share new science and healing tips as I learn. Photos of patients, places, and events from these stories can be found on Instagram.

Some of these healing stories may sound unbelievable, but science and historical data support the seemingly magical recoveries I describe. I wish you and your pets long, healthy lives!

MEET DR. DOUG COWARD

Dr. Doug Coward was born in Berkeley, California. He received his Bachelor of Science in Biology from the University of Santa Clara, a Master of Science in Animal Ecology, and a Doctor of Veterinary Medicine from the University of California at Davis. Upon graduation from Santa Clara, Dr. Coward played basketball for five years in Australia. He also coached the basketball team and taught biology at Haileybury College and did kangaroo parasite research at the Department of Tropical Veterinary Science at James Cook University. Dr. Coward traveled throughout Australia and then spent another year traveling and viewing wildlife in their natural habitats in New Guinea, Indonesia, Sri Lanka, India, Nepal, and Africa before veterinary school.

Dr. Coward did an internship with Dr. Thad Thorson, a renowned avian, reptile, exotic animal, and small animal dermatologist in Long Beach, California. In 1991, Dr. Coward replaced retiring avian and exotic animal specialist at the Animal and Bird Clinic of Mission Viejo, Dr. Perry Svedeen, and has never left.

Dr. Coward is a member of the American Association of Avian Veterinarians, Association of Holistic Veterinarians, Surfers Medical Association, Christian Veterinary Mission, and Academy of Human Integrative Health and Medicine.

Dr. Coward enjoys surfing every morning, attempting to pass his yoga teachers course started in Australia in 1976, and traveling with his wife Nancy, whom he met in Melbourne. They have two daughters and three grand-children who have all inherited the travel bug. He has spent over seven years working on this book project on animal and human health—including all the mistakes he has made and how to avoid them. Dr. Coward enjoys living near good waves in San Clemente, La Jolla, and Oahu.

PROLOGUE:

How a Surf-Stoked Veterinarian Flipped the Script on Animal Medicine

It was a typical foggy June-gloom morning in 2017. I struggled into my wetsuit, strapped my surfboard onto my rusty bike, and pedaled ten minutes to Trestles surf beach, near President Nixon's former San Clemente "Western White House." The bike path leading to the best year-round waves in the United States was unmarked, bordered on the east by Interstate 5 and on the ocean side by vegetation so dense you couldn't pass through without a machete. Layers of tightly packed plants and shrubs formed a wall of green, with enormous sycamore and willow trees dominating the canopy. The San Mateo Creek ran through the center of the forest, emptying into the ocean at Upper Trestles. The aroma was a blend of redwood forest and ocean spray. Later, I would learn that inhaling these plant fragrances, called phytoncides, was boosting my immune system and mood—a concept known as "forest bathing."

Until 1988, I had spent decades staying up until five thirty in the morning, cramming for exams in college and preparing lectures during the eight years I taught ecology, physiology, and zoology. Then my life changed. For the next four decades, I would leap out of bed at five thirty to plunge into the Pacific Ocean before sunrise. I became a member of the Dawn Patrol, the moniker for early rising surfers eager to catch waves before work.

I also learned about "earthing" after reading a *Sports Illustrated* article about quarterback Aaron Rodgers walking barefoot on the ground. This simple practice reduces inflammation and pain due to the interaction between the negatively charged ions on the earth's surface and our bodies. The earth acts as an antioxidant: reducing pain, improving sleep, promoting tissue repair, enhancing brain activity, and releasing feel-good endorphins. For Dawn Patrol surfers, the act of walking barefoot in the sand after biking through aromatic trees was an unknown health benefit, an unintentional gift that came with the pursuit of waves.

The foggy morning created a smooth, glassy ocean surface. The previous week's big swell had faded, but the waves were still substantial and perfectly shaped. I parked my bike on the deserted beach, stretched for a few minutes, then walked to the shore break and paddled into the chilly water. It was a glorious morning as the sun slowly rose over the Santa Margarita Mountains above Camp Pendleton Marine Base, burning away the fog. The ocean transformed from dark silver to deep blue, then to various shades of turquoise as the water coruscated brilliantly. The light show alone was worth getting up before dawn. It was magical. I caught fun waves, spotted a dozen Brandt's cormorants, playful bottlenose dolphins, and a plethora of brown pelicans flying gracefully in formation, their primary flight feathers just grazing the ocean's surface.

The dolphins appeared about thirty minutes after I paddled out. They came from the south, swimming toward me, and I assumed they'd continue north. There were four magnificent adults and two torpedo-like infants. To my amazement, they stopped and frolicked for about thirty minutes. I had never witnessed such joyful antics for so long in one place. I often saw dolphins while surfing, but they were always on the move, rarely stopping to catch a wave or two with exquisite grace and timing, unlike my clumsy efforts. Today, they leaped skyward in pairs, then plunged down nose-first, followed by their fluke fins, flapping and slapping the ocean gleefully. They repeated this playful routine numerous times. I stopped paddling for waves, mesmerized by their delight and amazing dexterity.

Suddenly, as a set wave arose, two adults separated from the group and headed straight toward me. Then they moved into perfect position to catch the wave. I paddled, glancing sideways to see the dolphins next to me, just two feet under the surface. As the wave crested and broke, they veered—one to the left, the other to the right—before leaping skyward, landing back into the wave's curl, and riding it for another ten yards. The moment was forever etched in my grateful mind.

Minutes later, my calves started cramping from the previous evening's hot yoga class. I had foolishly neglected to drink enough water. I watched more pelicans fly by, caught one last gentle wave, and rode it to the still-deserted beach.

I was full of joy, happy beyond reason as I caught that last wave. Surfers describe this blissed-out state as being "stoked." I call it my daily DOSE of Vitamin Sea, a term I use to describe the rush of brain chemicals—dopamine, oxytocin, serotonin, and epinephrine—generated by intense exercise in the ocean. The fragrance of the trees, the earthing effects of walking on the sand, and the immersive experience of being in the ocean had charged my body for the better. I was on my way to work, stoked and happy, despite any impending crises awaiting me in a profession ranked number one in suicide rates.

After surfing, I drove to our veterinary hospital in Mission Viejo, in the heart of the Saddleback Valley in Orange County, California. A friend had asked if their neighbor's daughter, Chantal, a pre-vet student at UC Berkeley, could shadow me for a day at the clinic. I agreed, out of nepotism. Berkeley was my hometown, and Cal was the university we grew up rooting for. Chantal was originally from India, where I had traveled for a month in 1979 and had also gotten married in the Himalayan village of Dharamsala, home to the Dalai Lama.

The clinic is always nonstop action, so I arranged to meet Chantal at the edge of our parking lot. She was waiting by her car, easy to spot in her Cal Berkeley blue and gold sweatshirt. After exchanging pleasantries and the customary school greeting of "Go Bears," we walked toward the front door. We didn't make it inside.

"Dr. Coward!"

It was Al and Marilyn Seargent, gesturing toward their German shepherd, Baron, lying quietly near them. I had known the couple for years and helped care for many of their German shepherds.

"Baron collapsed this morning. Last night, when he rolled over for a belly rub, I felt something like a bowling ball in his belly," Al said anxiously.

I bent down and lifted Baron's lips to examine his gums. They were white. I felt his femoral pulse. It was weak and rapid. Then I gently probed his abdomen and immediately found the "bowling ball." The huge abdominal mass was at least eight inches round. At the clinic, we saw patients in Baron's condition far too often. It was usually a tumor called a hemangiosarcoma that had ruptured, spilling blood into the abdominal cavity.

We immediately galvanized our staff into action. Our multitalented technicians, Juan and Rosa, quickly had Baron on a stretcher. Blood samples were drawn and processed in our lab. An IV catheter was inserted, intravenous fluids were given, and x-rays were taken. The abdomen was filled with blood, obscuring details, but an ultrasound provided a clearer view. The amorphous mass in the middle of the abdomen was hopefully attached to the spleen, which could be removed, and not part of the liver, which is too vital. Blood tests confirmed normal liver values, a very high white blood cell count (indicating infection, cancer, or both), and a dangerously low red blood cell count.

I explained to Chantal and the Seargents that we would stabilize Baron with fluids, antibiotics, vitamin B complex, and vitamin C before proceeding with exploratory surgery. After planning for the worst and a particularly bloody tumor removal, Baron's procedure went perfectly once the bleeding was stopped. Baron was stable and on the road to recovery.

Mondays are always manic in a veterinary clinic. Since we're closed on Sundays, we get the transfers from the local emergency clinic, along with patients who had been sick over the weekend but not sick enough to warrant an emergency visit. On top of that, we already had a full day of scheduled appointments, adding to the chaos. Fortunately, my first scheduled patient, an elderly terrier mix named Harry, had been dropped off that morning while I was in surgery.

I assumed the worst for Harry. At fifteen years old, he hadn't eaten in three days and hadn't had an exam in three years. Before I even laid eyes on him, I had braced myself for the possibility of advanced kidney disease or some other age-related ailment. But when I finally examined him, I was surprised. Harry was bright-eyed, energetic, and well-muscled, hardly the picture of a dog in decline.

A nose-to-tail exam revealed that everything was normal except for several infected, painful teeth. His blood work confirmed my suspicion: his organ function was excellent, but his white blood cell count was elevated, indicating a bacterial infection.

I met his owners, the Plumbs, in my exam room, which had floor-to-ceiling windows offering a much-needed connection to the outdoors during my long days inside. As I reviewed Harry's file before stepping in, I realized I had treated another one of their pets—a Dalmatian named Domino—years ago for bladder stones. But I had never seen Harry until today.

"Hi, Mr. and Mrs. Plumb. Sorry to keep you waiting," I said as they stood to greet me. They were both much older than me yet appeared as youthful and healthy as their dog.

"I have good news about Harry," I continued. "Based on his age and history of not eating, I was sure he had advanced kidney disease. But it turns out his organs are in great shape—his only issue is his teeth. It's hard to prevent dental infections in small dogs since they have the same number of teeth as a Saint Bernard but only half the space to fit them. The crowding leads to gingivitis and periodontal disease. Most of us can't brush our pets' teeth regularly, and I don't know anyone who flosses their dog's teeth, so infection is common. We'll start him on antibiotics now and schedule a dental cleaning later in the week, where we'll extract any decayed teeth. Honestly, I'm amazed at how great he looks."

Mr. Plumb chuckled. "Well, we're just doing for Harry what you told us to do for Domino. You told us to avoid kibble, so we started feeding both boys your diet suggestions of clean proteins and vegetables: healthy human food! They had so much energy and seemed so happy that we started eating the same way. And you know what? We feel great too. Harry's never been sick before, so we haven't had a reason to bring him in." He laughed again. "Friends keep telling us we look younger and healthier, and I tell them it's because we eat dog food now."

That got a hearty laugh out of me too.

We sent Harry home with antibiotics for the infection and probiotics to keep his gut microbiome balanced. It was another moment that reinforced what I had learned through years of experience—*real food has the power to heal, in animals and humans alike.*

The rest of the morning was a blur of diverse cases. We examined a feather-plucking parrot, a limping Labrador, an anorexic desert tortoise with a massive bladder stone, a vomiting golden retriever who had raided the trash, and a cheerful Australian shepherd who, in his excitement, wagged his tail and promptly sprayed diarrhea all over the exam room.

Lunch breaks in a veterinary hospital are never truly breaks. They're the time we handle elective procedures like spays and neuters, dental cleanings, and suturing up lacerations. By the afternoon, the pace finally slowed, with no more emergencies. At 7:30 p.m., we sat down for our first real meal of the day and locked the doors, just as Baron was discharged to the emergency clinic for overnight monitoring.

Then, right on cue, a minivan pulled into the driveway. One kid after another tumbled out, pounding on our door. Emma, our registered technician from Liverpool, took charge of the four kids while two adults emerged, cradling a young Vietnamese mini pig.

This was the typical finale to a day in veterinary medicine. We were all exhausted, our families had been calling for hours, dinner was cold, and yet here was another patient in need. And as every vet does, we unlocked the door, welcomed them in, and got to work.

The pig's name was Ham, and he was four months old, itching like crazy all weekend. His family had called dozens of clinics, searching for someone who treated pigs, until they were referred to us. They had driven over an hour from Los Angeles.

We're one of the few hospitals that treat any species that can fit through the front door.

Ham was too active to put on the exam table, so I knelt and examined him as his family crowded around, watching nervously. He was covered in dozens of red blotches. I gently scraped some inflamed skin from his back, placed it on a slide, and viewed it under the microscope.

The slide was teeming with mange mites—tiny, alien-looking creatures that burrow into the skin and cause unbearable itching.

I gave Ham a shot of ivermectin to kill the mites, and he let out an eardrum-rupturing scream. This was why most vets refuse to see pigs. At least Ham waited until I jabbed him. We advised the family to be careful handling him, as the mites could spread to humans.

Finally, the doors were locked for the last time. The day was over.

Chantal, the future veterinarian, practically vibrated with excitement. "This was the coolest day of my life! I have so many questions. Did you always know you wanted to be a vet? How hard is it to get into UC Davis? I've heard it's the best vet school in the world. And you're the first vet I've met who recommends people food for pets! I thought table scraps were bad, but you told every family how important real food is. Where did you learn that? And why don't other vets recommend it?"

I could only laugh. The ridiculously circuitous route that had led me to UC Davis, and later to this very moment, was nothing like what I had planned for myself. I had stumbled into veterinary school by pure serendipity. And it turned out to be the best thing I never planned to do.

Smiling, I told her, "It's a long story, full of disasters and unexpected turns. But I'll write it all down one day and send you a copy."

With that, I finally headed home. Late as usual.

PART ONE:
THE CIRCUITOUS
ROUTE

TO THE BEST JOB I PLANNED

NEVER TO DO

IN A PLACE I VOWED NEVER TO LIVE

CHAPTER 1

THE SHORT VERSION OF THE LONG STORY

Miracles do happen. In my forty years of practicing veterinary medicine, I've witnessed events that defy belief. Most stemmed from the magical healing properties of real food, while many others resulted from loving kindness mixed with modern medicine. However, they are all true, and these are the stories. I never imagined I would spend four decades indoors witnessing miracles when I was born with an innate desire to be outdoors, experiencing nature.

I was trained as an ecologist first and a wildlife veterinarian second, giving me a unique perspective on caring for animals. When I graduated from the University of California, Davis, School of Veterinary Medicine in 1985, I was the only student in my class of 120 who was committed from application to graduation to being a wildlife vet. Most of my classmates had decided to become animal doctors shortly after emerging from the womb. I, on the other hand, had never even met a veterinarian until I was twenty-five years old. My circuitous route to vet school began in Melbourne, Australia, where I played basketball after graduating from Santa Clara University in 1975. Seemingly unrelated events with three different veterinarians on three continents between 1978 and 1980 caused me to stumble into a profession I had vowed never to pursue, in a place I had vowed never to live, working indoors all day—which I had also vowed never to do.

The first veterinarian I met was at an expatriate Thanksgiving feast in Melbourne. During my first three years in Australia, I had little contact with Americans outside of basketball, as each team had one American player. Haileybury College, where I was head basketball coach and a biology instructor, had no Americans on the faculty. That changed when I met a blonde, free-spirited, blue-eyed Southern California girl who invited me to the feast. A mutual friend introduced us, knowing we both had pet parrots and California roots. Nancy, the blonde, was preparing for a grand adventure through New Guinea, Southeast Asia, Nepal, India, Afghanistan, and Iran, where she would eventually meet up with her sister. She had already backpacked around Europe, worked at a Bavarian ski resort, and taught high school in California before coming to Australia.

I also wanted to see more of the world, but in wild places where few travelers ventured. I enjoyed talking with her about her travels and the incredible ecosystems of California and Australia. Seated near me at the feast was an Aussie whose sister had married one of the American teachers. Inside my coat pocket was Sam, an impossibly cute baby nocturnal sugar glider possum, rescued from a cat's mouth by one of my biology students. I had offered to foster him until he was healthy enough to be released, though I had little clue what that would entail.

Sam suddenly woke up and repeatedly tried to jump onto the Aussie next to me. After dozens of attempts, he finally succeeded, landing on the man's arm. Unconcerned, the Aussie held up the sugar glider, examined him carefully, and greeted the creature with, "Ah, it's a little diprotodon. G'day, mate!" I apologized for Sam's bravado and asked what a diprotodon was. He explained it referred to the dental arrangement that allowed sugar gliders to dine on eucalyptus nectar. When I asked if he was a zoologist, he grinned and replied, "No, mate. I'm a wildlife veterinarian for the State of Victoria." I was fascinated by his tales of treating injured kangaroos, cockatoos, giant flightless emus, and wombats.

I soon forgot about the veterinarian, but I didn't forget about the blonde. After her trip around the world ended, she joined me for a yearlong adventure to see wildlife in wild places. She turned out to be the world's greatest backpack traveler. Nancy and I have now been married for forty-six years.

The second veterinarian I met was in Chitwan National Park in Nepal. We had left Australia in December 1978 to visit Indonesia, where we explored a UC Davis ecology study site in a remote Borneo jungle. I had applied to the UC Davis graduate program in ecology in 1975 but deferred it to play basketball in Australia. While in Borneo, we stalked orangutans in the jungle and then traveled to Sri Lanka, where we spent a month diving in pristine coral waters and searching for leopards. Our plan was to ferry across northern Sri Lanka into India and travel for several months, but a civil war in the north forced us to fly to Kathmandu instead.

On the plane, Nancy sat next to a talkative English girl who, upon learning we wanted to see wildlife, mentioned her part-time neighbor in Kathmandu: Dr. David Smith, a tiger researcher from the University of Minnesota. His study site was in Chitwan National Park, on the Indian border, and she thought he would be there for a few more months. I quickly wrote a letter asking if I could volunteer and gave it to the English girl to deliver.

We eventually made it down to the jungles of Chitwan after backpacking for two weeks on the Jomsom trail leading into Tibet. We were hiking up to our knees in snow one day and in a tropical jungle two days later after a number of harrowing bus rides on narrow roads on the sides of towering cliffs. We found Dr. Smith, and he said we were welcome to stay and help with his tiger ecology project. I had no idea if he ever received my letter. This was in 1979 and there was no internet, no telephone service, and little contact with the outside world.

We rode to the study site on the back of Asian elephants because the jungle grass was over six feet tall and rhinos were known to charge and maim anything that moved through the appropriately named elephant grass. An English ornithologist had recently met his fate at Chitwan by bird watching on foot and was flattened by a startled rhino. Our goal was to capture and radio-collar Sambar deer, the tigers' preferred prey. Another volunteer, a dapper Frenchman named Claude, joined us. When I struggled to restrain a deer that had slammed into the net, Claude yelled, "Kneel on him, like a horse!" I had no idea what he meant, as I had barely even seen a horse growing up in Berkeley.

"Look out!" Claude screamed as a hoof narrowly missed my head. He quickly restrained the deer with his knee like a seasoned professional. The deer had a bleeding gash above his eye. "Do you have vitamin K or C?" he asked me. I felt useless, having never packed such things. Dr. Smith soon arrived to collar the deer and set him free.

As we rode back to camp on an elephant, I asked Claude how he knew to kneel on the deer. "I'm a veterinarian," he said. "I work in Thailand, rehabilitating elephants. I didn't want to waste my life treating pampered poodles in Paris." I peppered him with questions about his work. When I mentioned my plans to study ecology at UC Davis, he became ecstatic. "UC Davis? Murray Fowler is there, the greatest wildlife vet in the world! I've read every word of his books!"

I explained that I planned to pursue a PhD in ecology, not veterinary medicine, but Claude continued praising UC Davis and Dr. Fowler. I soon forgot about Dr. Fowler but never forgot the adventure of riding on elephant back in the jungle. We continued our travels through India and Kenya, hitchhiking to game parks, seeing more wildlife than I had ever dreamed, and experiencing extraordinary hospitality along the way.

Looking back, my path to veterinary medicine was anything but traditional. Yet through every step—from the jungles of Borneo to the plains of Africa—one thing remained constant: nature's profound ability to heal. Whether in animals or humans, the best medicine is often the simplest: real food, time in the wild, and a life connected to the rhythms of the earth.

CHAPTER 2

THE ECOLOGICAL DISASTER IN DAVIS

While in Nairobi, I received a letter from UC Davis stating that I could begin my graduate studies in ecology in January 1980. UC Davis is a boutique, bucolic agricultural university, known worldwide for its winemaking school and veterinary school. I quickly settled into graduate school, sharing an office with two desert bighorn sheep researchers and loving both the coursework and camaraderie.

I was scheduled to meet with my graduate advisers for the first time in May. I had three advisers—two from the wildlife department, including the department head, Dr. Rawlings, and my primary adviser, Dr. Jake. The third adviser, oddly, was from the veterinary school. While I had met my wildlife advisers many times, I had never met the veterinarian, Dr. Joe Zinkl, until that meeting. I was looking forward to a friendly, introductory discussion led by my main adviser.

Instead, the head of the wildlife department immediately lit into me with a sarcastic rage, offering no greeting. Dr. Rawlings either hated Australians, basketball players, Jesuits universities, or all three, because he attacked my "pathetic background" with a fury I had never experienced. I thought my background was acceptable, even if I hadn't attended UC Davis as an undergraduate. Davis had a Division II basketball team, so I never considered going there. My goal was a Division I scholarship and, ultimately, a professional career in the NBA. I had been head of the biology department at Haileybury College. I had three years of teaching experience in biology, ecology, anatomy, and physiology. Before starting graduate school, I had seen hundreds of ecosystems around the world and thousands of wildlife species.

My fuse is normally quite long, but after ten minutes of this man's abuse, I struck back. I criticized his NRA-funded "Daffy Duck" research and the sycophantic graduate students who followed him around like waddling ducks. Dr. Rawlings glared at me, threw his chair down, and stormed out of the room. My primary adviser quickly followed, not even glancing my way.

The only adviser remaining was the veterinarian, whom I had just met. "I'm really sorry about what just happened, Dr. Zinkl. I usually don't behave that way. Dr. Rawlings really got under my skin."

"I'm just glad you didn't punch him like I thought you were about to," he replied with a smile. "Have you ever considered veterinary medicine, Doug? There's a wildlife track at the vet school run by a very charismatic veterinarian, Murray Fowler. I think you might enjoy that more than the wildlife department."

I burst out laughing, remembering Claude and Nepal—Claude couldn't stop raving about Murray Fowler. I quickly explained why I found the name so amusing.

Later that day, seeking to restore my equilibrium after the turbulent meeting, I took a quiet walk beneath the sprawling canopies on campus. The crisp air, the scent of wildflowers, and the soft chorus of birdcalls provided a healing respite from the academic storm, reinforcing my lifelong belief that clean nutrition and the natural world are the truest forms of medicine, not only for our patients but also for ourselves.

Dr. Zinkl would be the third wildlife veterinarian I met who ultimately redirected my future for the better. Dr. Zinkl offered to take me to the vet school the following day to show me the wildlife and zoological medicine department. The promise of exploring a field where nature's remedies are celebrated reinvigorated my passion, serving as a potent reminder that even in the midst of academic discord, nature remains the ultimate healer.

CHAPTER 3

DISCOVERING MY DHARMA IN THE EYE OF AN ELEPHANT

I didn't want to tell Dr. Zinkl that I had zero interest in becoming a veterinarian, stuck inside a clinic all day. But since he was the quintessential gentleman, I agreed to meet him at his office the next day for a visit to the "nondomestic/zoological animal ward." He mentioned that Dr. Fowler was on sabbatical for the year and that two other veterinarians would be overseeing the department in his absence.

The next morning, we walked ten minutes to the two-story veterinary teaching hospital, where I met the two gregarious veterinarians. They welcomed me warmly and asked if I could help load some gear into a van and assist them. We would be heading to the Sacramento Zoo for treatments, joined by two female vet students my age.

I had never been a big fan of zoos, but after witnessing so many animals up close in environments designed to mimic their natural habitats, my perspective shifted. I was captivated, not just by the animals but by the veterinarians themselves, working skillfully with primates, peacocks, parrots, and even polar bears.

Our last patient of the day was an Asian elephant, just like the ones I had ridden through the jungles of Chitwan

National Park in Nepal. He was tearing profusely from his right eye, which the students determined was due to an obstructed tear duct. A ladder was set up beside him so the vets and students could apply a fluorescein stain to check for corneal scratches. Then the vets demonstrated how to flush the tear duct using a lacrimal cannula, an improvised version made from a sterilized turkey baster. After the two students had their turn, Dr. Kolias, the veterinarian in charge, looked at me.

"Your turn."

I hesitated. "I'm just an ecology student—I've never used a cannula."

"Neither have we!" The vet students chimed in.

Dr. Kolias handed me the "lacrimal cannula" as I climbed the six-foot ladder. He guided me through the process, instructing me to insert the improvised instrument into the small depression in the elephant's swollen lower eyelid. As I flushed the eye with antibiotic solution, the elephant's gaze locked onto mine. A shiver ran up my spine. In that moment, I knew. I had found my dharma. I was meant to be a wildlife and zoological veterinarian.

From then on, my focus shifted. I quickly completed the few remaining classes I needed to apply to veterinary school, many of which overlapped with the coursework for a master's in ecology. I abandoned my original plan of pursuing a PhD in ecology, finished my master's requirements, and was thrilled to be accepted into veterinary school, which started in September 1981.

As my graduation date approached in June 1985, I reflected on the vows I had made to myself: I would never live in "sordid" Southern California, never be trapped indoors, and never, ever, be a pet vet. Yet, in all my planning, I had failed to consider one crucial detail: the job market for wildlife veterinarians was virtually nonexistent.

My dream had been to work outdoors, caring for California's sea otters, bighorn sheep, condors, mountain lions, coyotes, bobcats, and deer as the state's wildlife veterinarian. But that role was already filled—by a vet younger than me—who had once assured me he would never retire. He lied. He finally retired just a few years ago at age sixty-five.

My backup plan was to work as a wildlife veterinarian in one of the countries I had previously lived in or explored, places where animals still thrived in their natural ecosystems: Australia, New Guinea, Indonesia, India, Sri Lanka, Nepal, East Africa. I imagined myself in any of these wild landscapes, doing the work I felt called to do.

But reality, as I would soon learn, had other plans.

PART TWO: INTERNSHIP IN SORDID SOUTHERN CALIFORNIA

CHAPTER 4

I NEED A JOB THAT DOESN'T EXIST

I needed a real job, but there were none. I scoured the want ads in veterinary journals, searching in vain for anything involving wildlife. I looked everywhere: state and federal listings, universities, private practices known to see wildlife. Nothing.

Then Nancy picked up my copy of the *California Veterinary Medical Association* journal and found something I had completely overlooked. I had dismissed the "Mixed Animal" category, assuming those jobs were strictly rural—livestock, dairy, hogs, horses, sheep. That kind of life, far from the ocean and steeped in industrial agriculture, didn't speak to me. But the listing Nancy spotted, though misfiled under Mixed Animal, was anything but conventional. It was, in fact, a mixed practice, just not the sort I expected. This clinic treated wildlife, reptiles, birds, rabbits, rats, dogs, and cats. It should have been listed under Small Animal, a section I had already combed through with no luck.

The job was with Dr. Thad Thorson at Long Beach Animal Hospital. That name rang out like a bell. He had written a chapter in the latest *Current Veterinary Therapy* on dermatologic diseases of wildlife and exotic animals, a chapter I had practically memorized. During my fourth-year rotations in primate medicine, zoological medicine, and laboratory animal care, Dr. Thorson's insights had been a guiding light. His chapter had become my go-to reference for skin issues across species, from wildlife and zoo animals to birds and exotic pets.

I was first introduced to the importance of dermatology by Dr. Peter Irkle during my junior year. "Forty percent of your cases will involve the skin," he warned. "Stay awake in this class." He wasn't wrong. I found myself fascinated by the patterns: how similar the root causes of skin disease were across the six species we were trained to know well. Throughout my final clinical year, whenever I encountered a skin condition in a wild or zoo animal, I turned to Dr. Thorson's work. It was clear, methodical, and grounded in practical experience.

Nancy, a Cal State Long Beach graduate, knew the area well, especially the coastal town of Seal Beach, just next door. She also knew me well enough to recognize how strong my bias was against all things "SoCal." I was a proud Northern Californian, deeply skeptical of the south. To me, Southern California was a wasteland, ecologically compromised and culturally vacant. I'd repeated that refrain enough times to believe it myself. Overseas, when fellow travelers imagined California, they pictured palm trees, golden beaches, and bikini-clad blondes. I felt compelled to shatter those illusions by describing the summer fog in Berkeley, the frigid Pacific, and the scarcity of both sunshine and swimwear.

That disdain ran deep. I had been taught—explicitly and implicitly—that the thirty-third parallel marked a kind of Mason–Dixon Line in California, dividing the "enlightened north" from the water-stealing, philistine south. In the words of my field botany professor at Santa Clara, "Los Angeles is an ecological and cultural desert." I believed it. Yet, like most people who carry prejudice, I hadn't spent much time there. Truth be told, I knew India better than I knew Southern California. My only visits had been brief: passing through on my way to see my brother at UCSD or playing basketball games against teams like UCLA, USC, Loyola, and Pepperdine.

Still, something about the opportunity pulled at me. Maybe it was the wildlife. Maybe it was the idea of seeing the Mojave, the La Brea Tar Pits, Bristlecone pines, and Joshua trees, iconic landmarks I had long yearned to explore. Maybe it was the romantic hope of spotting gray whales off the Baja coast. Or maybe, as much as I hate to admit it, I saw Southern California as a testing ground, a place to make my rookie mistakes before returning north, more seasoned and with a checklist of ecological landmarks behind me.

The ad noted that Long Beach Animal Hospital was a teaching hospital, and the position was an internship. That meant long hours and low pay, but it also meant learning. I sent down my résumé.

I got the interview.

CHAPTER 5

THE PEG LEG PIRATE

The clinic sat on a busy corner, its bustle immediately evident. Separate entrances for dogs and cats hinted at thoughtful design, and the place hummed with activity. Every staff member wore matching khaki jumpsuits embroidered with *Critter Care* on the upper right pocket. I approached the reception desk and waited behind an elderly woman checking in with her rabbit, followed by a young boy and his mother bringing in a ball python. The place was unlike any clinic I'd ever visited.

I was soon escorted into a large office tucked deep within what felt like a maze. Doors branched off in every direction: toward the cat wing, treatment room, radiology, surgery, lab, a designated "snake room," the kennels, and a bathroom near the dog entrance. I was disoriented, to say the least. Debbie, the receptionist, a pre-vet student from Cal State Long Beach, navigated the labyrinth with ease. "Good luck with the interview," she said with a wry smile before disappearing behind one of the many doors.

Inside another expansive office, I met Merilee, the highly efficient and clearly well-organized office manager. She led me to a room lined with veterinary texts, everything from birds and snakes to dogs, cats, and small mammals, interspersed with volumes on natural history and regional field guides. "Doc will be in soon, once he's finished his morning rounds," she explained.

Plaques and certificates blanketed the walls—recognition from the Academy of Veterinary Allergy, the Academy of Veterinary Dermatology, and awards in zoological medicine. The room bore testament to decades of experience and expertise. I felt a wave of intimidation. My own résumé seemed paper-thin in comparison. I sat quietly, unsure if I belonged in such a place, thinking, *What am I doing here?*

Then I heard it: a rhythmic dragging sound, like a chair scraping slowly across the floor, growing louder as it approached. When the figure filled the doorway, I was momentarily stunned. A massive man stood there, about six feet, two inches tall, broad-shouldered, with long white hair slicked back, a matching beard and mustache, and twinkling eyes that gave him a boyish charm. He wore a short-sleeved khaki shirt with a *Critter Care* patch, similar in material to the staff uniforms, though clearly customized. Thick, burly arms extended from the sleeves, and a silver bracelet in the shape of a snake coiled around his left forearm. His pants were dark brown, his right leg whole, his left ending mid-thigh. Attached to that thigh was the source of the dragging sound: a carved mahogany peg leg.

He looked every bit the pirate—minus the parrot.

As he entered, I stood. "Dr. Coward, meet Dr. Thorson, better known as Doc," Merilee said.

"Well, howdy, Doug. Pleased to meet you," Doc said warmly. "Have a seat, 'cause I'm going to," he chuckled, settling into the chair behind the desk.

Merilee guided most of the interview. She asked about my veterinary training, where I grew up, and how I ended up in Australia. I explained that my move Down Under was a twist of fate, mostly a chance to continue playing basketball after my college career was sidetracked by fatigue and injuries. What followed was a brief stint teaching and coaching at Haileybury College, one of Melbourne's more prestigious schools.

Doc perked up when Australia came up. He asked whether I'd seen this snake or that lizard, bearded dragons, blue-tongued skinks, parrots of every kind. "Doc's both a herpetologist and a birder," Merilee added. "He's been to Australia several times."

Our conversation turned briefly to basketball. Doc displayed a surprising depth of knowledge for the game and admitted he was a Laker fan. Then Merilee mentioned she had called Dr. Murray Fowler, my mentor, and the reference I'd listed for wildlife medicine.

What came next nearly floored me.

"Dr. Fowler said you weren't worth paying a nickel," she said casually.

I sat in stunned silence. If the most respected wildlife and zoo veterinarian in the country thought I wasn't employable, my chances were shot. I slumped in my chair, head down, overwhelmed with despair. Our baby was due soon. I needed this job. In my mind, I was already planning my return to Australia, maybe a few more seasons of basketball in Perth or Brisbane while I searched for another veterinary opportunity.

The room went quiet. Doc broke the silence with a laugh. Then Merilee followed, chuckling as she explained: "Doc and Murray go way back. Doc was Walt

Disney's vet when Disneyland first opened and had a zoo. He also consulted for the San Diego Zoo on reptile care and feline vaccine protocols. They've been colleagues in zoo medicine for years."

She continued, "Murray always said Davis grads weren't worth paying for six months because they lacked hands-on experience. But he also said you'd be just fine, eventually. He trained you himself for two years, after all."

Relief washed over me. I exhaled and felt my pulse begin to slow.

Merilee then gave me a full tour of the sprawling hospital. One large room was dedicated to Doc's personal snake collection. Another room housed a cat colony used for nutrition research. Doc was studying dietary causes of feline lower urinary tract disease, a common and potentially fatal condition in male cats caused by blockages in the urethra. Crystals, epithelial cells, and sometimes bacteria would obstruct the flow of urine, backing toxins into the bloodstream and quickly leading to nausea, collapse, and death if not relieved.

I recalled one of our kidney professors' crude but effective analogy: "How would you men like it if the treatment for your urinary blockage was to whack your penis off?" That, unfortunately, was often the go-to veterinary solution at the time: perineal urethrostomy. But Doc was approaching it differently. According to Merilee, he was close to solving the issue through dietary changes alone. It was the first time I'd encountered the idea of treating a surgical condition with food as medicine—and it wouldn't be the last.

The hospital included a fully equipped surgery suite, radiology room, and an in-house lab where Doc cultured skin, urine, and ear samples, then ran sensitivity panels to select the most appropriate antibiotics. He maintained a custom-designed avian and reptile ward, kept at a consistent 90°F to optimize healing for his ectothermic patients.

Doc had two certified animal health technicians, our profession's equivalent of registered nurses, both highly skilled. I was genuinely impressed. Merilee showed me a long list of procedures Doc regularly performed on his "critters," as he affectionately called them. The scope of his surgical abilities was staggering.

"Doc desperately needs help," Merilee said, "but he's picky. A perfectionist. He wants things done his way. The last new vet lasted two weeks before Doc booted him out." I was surprised. Doc had seemed easygoing in our brief conversation. But one thing stuck in my mind. I wanted to ask about the peg leg. I just couldn't bring myself to do it.

"This is a teaching hospital," Merilee continued. "The internship won't pay much. You'll work long hours. No moonlighting. Doc wants you fresh and eager to learn. He's brilliant, and this is a rare opportunity to work with someone truly exceptional."

I signed on the spot. I started the week after graduation.

We found a tiny apartment in Seal Beach, just a block from the ocean and a ten-minute walk from the pier and library. My Southern California adventure was about to begin.

Little did I know just how long that adventure would turn out to be.

Chapter 6

My First Patient Is a Skunk

On the first morning of my veterinary career, I met with Doc for what he called our daily "huddle"—a pre-appointment roundup of all hospitalized patients. Before the first client walked through the door, we visited each recovering animal: snakes coiled quietly in their warm enclosures, parrots preening in soft light, dogs and cats curled in kennels, and a rat with a healing abscess. Accompanying us were two of the clinic's highly skilled veterinary technicians, who reviewed each patient's treatment plan, appetite, and even the character of their urine and stools with thoughtful precision.

As we stepped away from the last cage, Doc turned to me with a mischievous grin and declared, "There's the right way, the wrong way, the UC Davis way, and then there's my way. We do things my way." I nodded, silently grateful to have any guidance at all.

Doc continued, warming to his favorite subject. "Whatever they taught you in Dermatology is wrong. They're treating the skin from the outside in. We treat from the inside out. Skin is a beautiful window into the whole animal. You have to understand what's going on beneath the surface. Allergies to pollen make up half of what you'll see. Another quarter will be tied to diet regarding food allergies, sensitivities, and poor nutrition. The rest are parasites, environmental toxins, or organ dysfunction that manifests on the skin. So we work from the ground up. Start with blood work: rule out infection, assess internal organ function, and test urine. Then we do the basic skin diagnostics: scraping, cytology, a Wood's lamp, and DTM culture. And no steroids until every single piece of the puzzle is in front of us."

It was a lot to take in. I'd sat through the standard dermatology lectures during my third year and had absorbed the basics, like everyone else. But I'd skipped the dermatology rotation at the teaching hospital in favor of more exotic animal work, where skin issues were less common. Most of what I remembered boiled down to one key idea: when in doubt, prescribe steroids to stop the itching. Clearly, Doc was playing a different game entirely.

I confessed my inexperience, expecting a frown. But Doc just chuckled. "Good," he said. "That means you've got nothing to unlearn. Around here, we do dermatology tests on everything that walks, slithers, or flies."

Our first patient that morning was a skunk named Petunia.

Petunia arrived in a blue cat carrier, escorted by her young, soft-spoken owner, Rachael. It was my first day wearing the official Critter Care lab coat, and I felt both proud and slightly ridiculous as I followed Doc into the exam room. "Howdy do! What have we here?" Doc said, peering into the carrier.

"This is Petunia," Rachael replied with a Georgia drawl. "I got her as a baby. She was de-scented before I adopted her—legal and all. But she's been scratching like crazy, and no one out here seems to know what to do. The bald spot's getting bigger, and every vet I've seen said to come to you."

Doc opened the carrier and gently guided Petunia onto the exam table. "That's a good girl," he said softly, running a practiced hand down her flank. The hairless lesion on her back was about the size of a half-dollar, angry, red, and unmistakably inflamed. He spent several minutes examining her from nose to tail, murmuring soothing words while he worked. I had never seen a skunk up close, let alone one this tame.

"Well, Rachael," Doc said at last, "I can't tell you what's wrong by looking, but I know how to find out." Rachael looked visibly relieved. "The other vets were afraid to touch her, even after I told them she was de-scented."

Doc began collecting samples with swift, confident motions: a piece of clear tape pressed to the skin for surface cells; a skin scraping with a blade; a few hairs plucked from the lesion's edge. All the while, he kept up a calm and casual conversation with Rachael.

"Dr. Doug here's going to check for bacteria, yeast, allergy cells, and mites," he said, handing me the samples. "The hair goes into a DTM culture to check for ringworm—a fungal infection. If it's there, the medium will turn red and sprout white fuzzy colonies. And we'll use a Wood's lamp because sometimes ringworm glows under UV light."

He asked me to flip the lights off while he held the Wood's lamp over Petunia's back. "And looky here!" he said, as a vivid green fluorescence lit up the lesion and nearby fur. "We've got a dermatophyte on our hands."

Doc glanced at me. "Now, go check that slide and see what else might be lurking."

In the back treatment room, I settled in at the microscope. I'd performed fecal and skin analyses hundreds of times during vet school, but this was the real world, and the slide was for Doc. I felt the pressure. Under high power, I spotted neutrophils, which are multilobed immune cells that are first on the scene in inflammation, and a few eosinophils, hinting at possible allergies or parasites. An occasional purple dot, likely Staphylococcus bacteria, rounded out the picture. I asked Karen, one of the senior techs, to double-check. She laughed. "Doc already told me to follow up after the rookie!"

Back in the exam room, Doc was instructing Rachael on how to bathe Petunia using a pungent lime sulfur shampoo. "Wear gloves," he cautioned. "Ringworm's zoonotic—it can spread to people." Rachael rolled up her sleeves to reveal several red, coin-sized lesions on her arms. "I figured it might be related," she said sheepishly.

"I only treat primate monkeys, not people," Doc quipped with a grin. "But you might want to let your doctor know what Petunia's carrying."

Tears welled in Rachael's eyes. "Thank you, Dr. Thorson. She's all I've got from home, my little piece of Georgia out here."

As we returned Petunia to her carrier, I felt a wave of gratitude. For the medicine, yes—but also for being in a place where we treated the whole animal, where nature wasn't a backdrop but a guide, and where healing came from understanding. Not just from drugs, but from food, light, warmth, and touch.

Doc and I scrubbed our arms with Betadine. My hands smelled like sulfur and iodine, but I didn't care. I was in the right place. The real work had begun.

CHAPTER 7

LESSON 1—THE KISS PRINCIPLE

There was never a dull moment with Doc. In the course of a single day, we might examine turtles, tarantulas, goldfish, monkeys, pythons, rabbits, rats. And, of course, a variety of dogs and cats. We saw everything from skin disease to vomiting, diarrhea, fractures, diabetes, and beyond. Yet no matter the patient, Doc never varied his approach. His philosophy was simple: find out what's actually wrong and treat *that*. Not what might be wrong. Not what could be wrong. Just the truth, as directly and thoroughly as possible.

He constantly reminded us to follow the KISS principle. At first, I thought I must've missed that lecture in school. So I asked Karen, the lead technician, "What's the KISS principle Doc keeps mentioning?"

Karen burst out laughing. "For us it means 'Keep It Simple, Sweetheart.' For you, it means 'Keep It Simple, Stupid.' But Doc's too polite to say that part out loud. We're not."

Everyone had noticed my hesitation when it came to recommending tests that could be costly. Having lived on as little as three dollars a day while traveling through India and Southeast Asia, I understood the value of a dollar in a very real way. During the summer of 1984, I worked on the Navajo reservation gaining large-animal experience, where 90 percent of our cases had to be treated without diagnostics. We had no choice—we worked with what we had.

So I arrived at Critter Care with the mindset that you treated symptoms first and ran tests later, if needed. Doc, however, gently corrected that line of thinking. "Our job is to help heal, not to pass judgment on someone's finances," he said. "You give people the option. Let them decide what level of care they're comfortable with. You have *no idea* how much these critters mean to their families. I offer the best because it's the simplest and fastest way to heal. If you can find the problem, you can choose the right treatment. Otherwise, you're just guessing, and guessing can lead to harm."

He paused, then added with a grin, "Except in dermatology. With skin, it's *my way or no way*. There are fifteen different diseases that can look the same, and one disease can look fifteen different ways. We *must* run tests in derm cases." He gave me a reassuring pat on the back. "Don't worry. Let the clients decide. Just offer them the truth."

Lesson 2—Thou Shall Not Judge

Later that afternoon, Doc was elbow-deep in a ferret fracture repair when a high school teacher named Eric walked in with his coughing Labrador retriever. Without missing a beat, Doc said, "Pretend you're me and go see the dog."

It would be my first solo patient.

I walked into the exam room and introduced myself. Eric, who looked a few years older than me, had a neatly trimmed black beard and a calm presence. Moses, his chocolate Lab, wagged his tail enthusiastically and looked up at me with warm golden eyes. He was eight years old and had started coughing about a week earlier.

I began my exam. His heart rate was a normal 124 beats per minute. No murmurs—his valves were tight and quiet. His lungs sounded clear. I gently palpated the trachea to check for irritation; dogs with kennel cough often erupt in a sharp cough when pressure is applied. But Moses didn't flinch. I palpated his abdomen, and he turned and licked me in the face.

"I guess that doesn't hurt," Eric said with a smile.

Everything felt normal, but I still didn't have a diagnosis. A cough could mean anything. Heartworm, bronchitis, cancer, pneumonia, even allergies. I remembered Doc's words: offer the best and fastest way to find the *cause.*

I explained to Eric that Moses might have a bacterial or viral lung infection, or perhaps a heart condition causing fluid to back up in the lungs. Another possibility was heartworm. If Moses had been bitten by a mosquito carrying larvae, the worms could have grown in his heart. I had seen hundreds of dogs with heartworm while working in a parasitology lab at James Cook University in tropical Townsville, Australia. Some were so weak they could barely cross the street; others had only a mild cough.

Eric asked how we could find out for sure.

"We can do a chest x-ray to check the lungs and heart, and a blood test to rule out heartworm and look for infection."

"You can do all that *right now?*" he asked.

"Yes," I replied. "It'll take about an hour."

"An hour? That's it?" Eric was stunned. "It takes *weeks* for my doctor to get x-rays and test results!"

I explained that we had our own lab and x-ray facilities, and we got to work. Karen drew blood from Moses, who continued wagging and charming the whole staff. She passed the blood through a circular filter to screen for microfilaria, baby heartworms, but found none under the microscope.

Meanwhile, Tess spun the blood in the centrifuge and prepped for x-rays. Moses lay on his side, then his back, tail thumping all the while. Tess developed the films in the darkroom while Karen examined the blood smear, counting white blood cells to help determine whether we were dealing with a bacterial or viral infection.

When Tess returned with the films, she clipped them onto the light viewer. The heart looked normal. No enlargement, no fluid backup. But the lungs were littered with small donut-shaped shadows. These rings indicated thickened, inflamed bronchi. Instead of clean, air-filled airways, the bronchi were clogged with inflammatory cells.

The last piece of the puzzle came from the blood work. Moses's white cell count was 21,000, well above the normal range of 6,000 to 18,000. That meant we were likely looking at a bacterial infection. Neutrophils, the immune system's first responders, flood the bloodstream during a bacterial assault, just like Marines arriving on the front lines.

As Doc finished the ferret's fracture repair, he reviewed the results. "Looks like bacterial bronchitis to me," he said. "Let's treat with antibiotics and a little Robitussin DM."

Then he looked at me with a twinkle in his eye. "Remember—DM stands for *Dog Medicine.*"

By the time we'd given Moses an antibiotic injection and dispensed a ten-day prescription, the hour had passed. Eric was overjoyed. He told me that his last dog had died of lung cancer. It had started with a cough, just like Moses.

As I showed him the x-rays, I explained that the donut-shaped shadows were most likely due to inflammation, not cancer. Doc popped into the room to say hello and check for any lingering questions.

"Nope," Eric said. "You were fantastic. I can't believe how fast and thorough everything was. Thank you so much, Dr. Thorson, and Dr. Doug. Moses is my best friend. I don't know what I'd do if I lost him."

After Eric left, Doc turned to me and said, "That's why we treat the cause, not the symptoms."

I nodded, taking it all in. He was a specialist and there was a rhythm to this work, something elemental and grounded, like reading tracks in the dirt or watching the weather shift. It wasn't just science. It was observation. Pattern recognition. The wisdom of slowing down, listening closely, and letting nature speak. And more often than not, it did.

CHAPTER 8

NEW DAD, NEW CAREER

Our daughter Kelly was born in January 1986, right in the thick of my internship. She was pure delight, sunshine bundled in soft pajamas. From the start, she loved being outside. We'd stroll along the Seal Beach pier, watching sea birds skim the waves, surfers bobbing in the swell, swimmers splashing in the shallows, and families just enjoying the day. Her very first word was "walk." It fit her perfectly.

Our tiny apartment had just enough space for the three of us. Money was tight. My internship paid $22,000 a year, which worked out to about two dollars an hour, given that I worked from 8:00 a.m. to 7:00 p.m. six days a week. Sundays were my only days off. Still, we made it work. What we lacked in income, we made up for in sunlight, sea air, and that sense of starting something real.

One saving grace was the long midday break. I used to think Doc just took his time at lunch, but there was more to it than that, something I'd come to understand later. As soon as I got off at noon, I'd rush home to Seal Beach. The three of us would grab towels and head straight to the ocean. Nancy would float on her back while I played with Kelly in the waves, then we'd switch. Thirty minutes in the saltwater with my little family gave me enough joy and perspective to head back indoors for the afternoon. Doc made sure I could get home nearly every lunch hour, and I've always been grateful for that. I heard horror stories of interns who never saw daylight for twelve months straight. That would've pushed my NDD, nature deficit disorder, beyond repair. Without those morning beach walks and lunchtime doses of vitamin sea, I might've left private practice altogether.

During those early months, I still planned to pursue a residency in zoological and wildlife medicine. My dream had always been to become a state wildlife veterinarian or work at a zoo. Doc, of course, had strong opinions about this.

"You'll end up working for a paper-pushing administrator who doesn't know the first thing about animal care," he told me one afternoon, looking over his glasses. "Unless you're lucky enough to get into the San Diego Zoo, which actually gets it right, your skills will be wasted. Everywhere else, you won't be able to help the critters unless some bureaucrat signs off on it. Their priority is public viewing, not animal health. And the most satisfying part of this job is using what you spent four years learning—interpreting blood work, reading x-rays, doing surgery, and figuring out exactly what's wrong so you can heal it."

I wondered if Doc was just being cynical. He clipped articles from journals and newspapers to prove his points, always with a bit of flair. But his words stuck with me. My dream of becoming board-certified in zoological medicine began to shift. I had a new dream now, one that looked a lot like Kelly's tiny hand gripping my finger.

If I pursued a residency, I'd be working eighty hours a week, and I'd miss it all. The walks. The waves. Her first words. Her first steps.

In early 1988, just a few months after Kelly was born, I made the decision. I picked up the phone and called the four programs I'd applied to. I withdrew my applications. A few days later, Dr. Murray Fowler, one of the founding figures in zoo medicine, called me personally.

"I'm glad you chose fatherhood over a residency," he said. "I've got five kids. You won't regret it."

It was a quiet moment of affirmation. I had once vowed, at twenty, never to marry, never to take on a mortgage, never to be tethered to children. Now here I was: married, broke, and hopelessly in love with a blonde-haired baby girl.

And I felt like the richest man in California.

Chapter 9

Go Bend an Elbow

Doc was a passionate seeker of knowledge and loved going to continuing education (CE) meetings. After six months of training me, he hoped I wouldn't destroy his iconic practice in his absence and headed off to Minnesota for a conference. His new hobby, bird watching, was gaining momentum. Lately, he had started planning his CE trips around rare bird sightings. He always attended the annual allergy, dermatology, avian, and reptile meetings, but now he was adding smaller weekend conferences in prime birding locations.

Doc hadn't had an associate vet in four years, and he was eager to travel again, provided the practice didn't fall apart while he was gone. He encouraged me to follow the same path in my career. "You learn just as much bending an elbow before and after the meetings as you do at the meetings," he advised. When I admitted I didn't know what he meant, he chuckled and pantomimed bringing a drink to his lips. "I've learned more unsolicited practice tips in bars than in lecture halls," he said with a wink.

The first time Doc ventured off, I was terrified. He told me to call his friend, Dr. Perry Svedeen in Mission Viejo, an hour south of Long Beach, if I needed help. "He's the best bird and exotic vet in Southern California," Doc said.

The very next morning, with Doc off birding, I met Tracy and her cocker spaniel, Charlie, who had been referred for chronic itching. Tracy was waiting in the exam room with a look of exasperation and a reeking dog in her lap.

"Charlie's on so many drugs. He looks miserable. He reeks worse than my son's socks, and that's saying something. I can't stand to see him suffer. Oh, and I was told the skin doctor has a peg leg. You couldn't be him," she said, sizing me up.

She looked like she'd been born on a surfboard, sun-kissed blonde hair, athletic, confident. Her disappointment in me was palpable.

I got that look a lot. Clients expecting the peg-legged pirate of dermatology were often underwhelmed by my thirty-two-year-old baby face. Many flat-out asked to see "someone more experienced." They weren't wrong. Most of my peers had six years' experience by this point. I was playing catch-up.

I reassured Tracy that Doc was away continuing his derm education and would be back later in the week. I explained that I'd do the initial workup and Doc would take it from there. I took Charlie's history, performed a skin scrape and cytology, drew blood, and talked about food trials and potential allergy testing.

I could practically recite Doc's derm workup by heart by now. Typically, I handled the first thirty minutes of the exam while Doc was next door treating an egg-bound parrot or a constipated iguana. Then he'd join me, saving the day, and the case. I didn't mind being second string to Doc. It was like riding the Lakers bench behind Hall of Famer Jerry West. I was learning from a master.

But today there was no Doc, and Charlie smelled like he'd rolled in mounds of dog poop. Under the microscope, I found no mites, but I did find neutrophils and clusters of little purple balls, likely Staph bacteria. The techs ran blood and urine tests while I discussed diet and the foods Doc would recommend for an allergy trial as well as gentle antibacterial shampoos. I promised Tracy that we'd call her as soon as Doc returned.

When he did, Doc motioned for me to join him in the back to review Charlie's results.

"Well, Doug, how should we treat ol' Charlie?" he asked.

"Uh, well … there's Staph on cytology, the skin is lichenified and hypopigmented. He's probably hypothyroid. He'll need antibiotics for three to six weeks, at least through the food trial. I'm not sure what to do about the itching since we don't use steroids," I said nervously.

Steroids were the go-to treatment for itching, but they wreaked havoc with long-term use—damaging joints and the liver, making dogs drink like camels and urinate like horses. Still, I didn't know what else would stop Charlie's misery.

"Looky here," Doc said, pointing at the blood work. The white blood cell count was elevated, no surprise given the infection. But his eosinophils, which are often elevated in allergies, were normal. That was strange. His thyroid was also normal.

Then we saw it. Charlie's liver enzymes were through the roof. Everything else looked fine. Doc explained that dogs treated with repeated rounds of steroids often developed elevated liver values. He believed Charlie's liver had been overworked, and now it was failing to detoxify the body, contributing to his rancid skin.

"Heal the liver, heal the skin," Doc said simply.

I'd never made that connection before. I thought of the advice we'd shared while backpacking through India: brown skin and yellow urine was fine. But yellow skin and brown urine meant hepatitis or liver disease. Charlie wasn't yellow, but his liver was clearly distressed.

We called Tracy and scheduled a recheck. She was thrilled to see the peg-legged vet this time. "Howdy, Tracy," Doc said, with his usual warmth. "We've got what we need to help Charlie."

He explained the plan: a prescription diet with a "novel" protein, unlikely to trigger allergies, and designed to support liver function. He added liver supplements to promote detox and regeneration, a course of antibiotics, and a special shampoo.

"But what about his allergies?" Tracy asked. "Every vet says cockers just have terrible allergies."

Doc smiled. "Right now, we're healing his liver and skin. If he's still itching in a few weeks, we'll reassess. Sound fair?"

"I'll do whatever you say," she said. "I wasn't so sure when I saw Dr. Doug. He needs some gray hair to look smarter." She winked at me, thankfully without malice.

I couldn't wait to see Charlie in a month. The receptionist checked in weekly. Progress was steady but not dramatic. Just "a little better." But when Charlie walked into the clinic for his recheck, I was stunned: He didn't smell. His skin had lost the dark, wrinkled, greasy look called lichenification. His coat was soft and shiny. The hyperpigmentation from chronic skin disease was gone. He was bouncing around like a puppy. And Tracy was beaming.

"Thank you, Dr. Thorson! Charlie's back. I thought I was going to have to put him down. He's my best friend. Everyone who knows me knows Charlie is *numero uno*."

She gave Doc a huge bear hug, and me a polite hand-shake, then one more hug for Doc on the way out.

"I told you," Doc said, smiling. "Heal the liver, heal the skin."

He had figured that out years earlier by always starting with his full dermatology panel and treating the actual results, not just guessing like I would have. If it had been up to me, I would've given Charlie steroids and pushed his liver over the edge. He'd have ended up yellow, itchy, urinating brown buckets, and Tracy would've lost her best friend. And probably punched me in the nose.

CHAPTER 10

DOC CONVERTS ME

After two years, Doc asked me if I'd take over his practice. He wanted to retire and travel. I couldn't imagine seeing all the patients he managed to see in a day, especially with a peg leg and well into his sixties. I also didn't want to settle in Southern California. My DNA cried out for the redwood trees of the north. I thanked Doc and told him I wasn't ready yet.

I had been enjoying my apprenticeship. I stayed on well beyond the original one-year internship, still earning the same minimal wage. Doc was that generous of an instructor, and a true master of his multispecialty craft. In addition to his legendary expertise in avian, exotic, and reptile care, Doc introduced me to the mysterious and often mind-boggling world of dermatology in dogs, cats, and birds.

I became a dutiful acolyte, quickly learning Doc's creed: "There's the right way, the wrong way, the UC Davis way … and my way. We'll do it MY WAY!"

Eventually, I mustered the courage to ask about his leg. Merilee quietly told me Doc had lost it on Okinawa, his first day in combat during WWII. He lived with constant pain from the war wound. His two-hour lunch breaks weren't for leisure, as I'd always thought. They were for lying down and easing the pain. He never once mentioned it. He never complained. He just grinned, laughed often, and taught tirelessly. When one of my cases went sideways, he didn't scold. He simply offered a gentle shrug and said, "That's why we call it practice."

To my utter surprise, I found joy indoors at my first job in a veterinary hospital. Doc's mentorship turned what I thought would be a short detour into a lifelong path. Letting go of my dream of a wildlife residency turned out to be a gift. I had stumbled into a side of veterinary medicine I had never considered and have now continued to love for more than four decades.

Inside those animal hospitals, I discovered something sacred: a tribe of passionate healers. A team of people so devoted, they couldn't imagine doing anything else. They welcomed new puppies and kittens. They consoled grieving families. They answered lifestyle questions for a dozen different species. They diagnosed discomfort using blood work, x-rays, ultrasounds, and educated intuition. They gave medications by injection, by mouth, by rectum, by IV. They performed hundreds of surgeries on dozens of species. And they did it all with gentle pats, whispered words, and quiet compassion—*for both ends of the leash*.

Thanks to Doc and his staff, I came to love the excitement, energy, and joy of companion animal medicine. It's a world full of humor, heart, and harmony.

And so, I must now confess: I've reneged on all three vows I made in my twenties.

I married.

I took on a mortgage.

I raised a daughter.

And I've spent forty years in Southern California, working ten to fourteen hours a day indoors ... as a "pet vet."

CHAPTER 11

WAITING IN PARADISE

L ife couldn't have been any better. Ten years earlier, I would never have imagined saying that. At the time, the two things I feared most were marriage and a mortgage. Fatherhood wasn't even on the radar. But now, the girls amplified everything that was good in life. These were happy times.

Our second daughter, Shawn, was born exactly two years after Kelly. With the ecological landmarks of Southern California now checked off my list, I turned my eyes north once again, back toward the towering redwoods and eco-paradise. I decided to seek a partnership in an existing practice and began focusing on the Monterey Bay Area, a place we both loved for its incomparable beauty: the rugged coastlines, the misty mountains of Big Sur, and the comfort of having our families nearby.

I launched a letter-writing campaign to see if any veterinarians were nearing retirement and looking for a partner. A few months later, I received a reply from one of the first vets to practice in the Monterey area. He was thinking of retiring in a few years and had a younger partner who didn't want to run the whole clinic alone. They welcomed the idea of a new partner. It was a perfect fit for Nancy and me. We still had adventures to pursue in Southern California, the girls were enthusiastic little travelers, and I still had so much to learn. We began traveling frequently to the clinic, perched on the edge of Pebble Beach, Monterey, and Carmel, to meet the partners and envision our future.

On my one day off each week, we often drove south to Laguna Beach. It was full of life and reminded me of Berkeley more than any other part of Southern California, with its vibrant mix of artists, environmental activists, poets, surfers, businesspeople, and dreamers all coexisting. There were galleries to wander through and stretches of preserved coastal land open to the public. The ocean water was clear and inviting, with pristine coves perfect for snorkeling and miles of public parks. At Main Beach, volleyball and basketball players provided a constant show for tourists and locals alike.

Coastal South Orange County began to feel like home. It echoed the natural spirit of Northern California but with a warmer, more welcoming Pacific Ocean, not as fierce or untamed as the one I had grown up beside. Just south of Laguna was San Clemente, the epicenter of Southern California surf culture, home to the region's surf magazines and lifestyle.

Nancy introduced me to San Clemente right around the time Doc was preparing to sell his practice. She had visited the town many times as a child and always loved its charm. Compared to Laguna, San Clemente was a quiet beach community with a small-town feel. The main street sloped gently down to a long wooden pier. We walked south from the pier along pristine sand, marveling at the crystal-clear water, uninterrupted by oil derricks like those off Seal Beach. In the distance, Catalina Island shimmered on the horizon, while a nearby rocky outcrop teemed with sea lions. Wild Amazon parrots screeched from the palm trees above, their emerald feathers flashing in the sun. The beach was nearly deserted except for a few surfers. It reminded us of the untouched coastlines we'd seen in Australia—the parrots in the trees, soft sand beneath our feet, and hardly a footprint in sight.

That day, we decided spontaneously to move to San Clemente while we waited for the Carmel vet to retire. Those were truly halcyon days, before the catastrophe that lay ahead.

I began looking for work in South Orange County and quickly found opportunities. Several veterinary clinics in Laguna Beach, San Clemente, Laguna Niguel, and San Juan Capistrano were happy to have me cover one or two days a week, allowing their owners a rare break in the middle of the week. I became a "relief veterinarian," floating from practice to practice.

At the same time, I reached out to the biology department at Saddleback College in Mission Viejo and inquired about part-time teaching opportunities. Their paramedic program needed someone to teach Anatomy and Physiology. They had been looking for a physician but hadn't found one, so they settled on me, an animal doctor, but a passionate teacher nonetheless.

To top it off, I wandered into the Saddleback Valley Emergency Hospital and was greeted by a familiar face: a former classmate from UC Davis. He was now managing the emergency clinic and in need of help at night. I joined their rotation, working two to three evenings a week.

The Saddleback Valley group was exceptional: young, forward-thinking, and equipped with state-of-the-art technology. Each vet had a specialty they loved and generously shared their knowledge. They also knew I was preparing to enter a partnership, so they offered invaluable insights into the business side of practice ownership, a realm still foreign to me.

By 1988, we had settled happily in San Clemente, soaking in this beautiful chapter of life. The senior veterinarian in Carmel was expected to retire in 1991, and we looked forward with cautious optimism to that transition.

We had no idea that the disaster of 1991 was already beginning to stir.

CHAPTER 12

CATASTROPHE

I was suturing up the throat of a rooster that had been attacked by a coyote late at night on April 6, 1991, at the emergency clinic when I got the phone call that changed my life.

I had recently learned avian throat surgery from bird surgeon Dr. Perry Svedeen, whom Doc admired and knew well. Dr. Svedeen had founded the Animal and Bird Clinic of Mission Viejo in 1975 as a specialty hospital for birds as well as other small animals. I had walked into his tiny, aging clinic one afternoon to ask if he needed relief work. The receptionist didn't hesitate: "He needs help this minute. Otherwise I'll be answering the phone while assisting in surgery. Just walk in and introduce yourself."

So I stepped into surgery and introduced myself to Dr. Perry Svedeen. Wiry and cheerful, he was in his fifties and had a red-tailed hawk wrapped tightly in a towel on the table.

"My tech called in sick, and I could use a hand to devocalize this hawk, if you've got an hour to spare," he said without missing a beat.

He explained that the hawk flew as part of the dinner entertainment at Medieval Times, but screeched loudly in its handler's apartment all day long, so much so that the handler was facing eviction unless the hawk could be silenced.

"I'm the only one who does this surgery," Dr. Svedeen said. "If you learn it, maybe I can finally retire."

The hawk needed anesthesia, and Dr. Svedeen asked me to inject a preloaded syringe into its pectoral muscle. While the bird drifted off to sleep, he outlined the delicate surgery on a scrap of paper.

Dr. Fowler had once taught us that devocalization was both cruel and anatomically impossible due to the proximity of the vocal apparatus, the syrinx, to the heart. I mentioned this to Dr. Svedeen.

"I invented the surgery for situations just like this," he said. "Euthanizing a healthy bird over noise never sat right with me. I've devocalized the peacocks at Hugh Hefner's mansion, a dozen raptor species, even pet chickens who turned into crowing roosters. I'm a falconer too, so falconry folks refer birds to me from all over California."

He explained that the surgery was incredibly risky. "I have to blindly cauterize the syrinx beneath the trachea, which sits right next to the beating heart. Cauterize too much, they die. Nick the heart, they die. If I don't cauterize enough, they're back to screaming in three weeks."

He worked while I monitored anesthesia and handed him instruments. Soon the trachea was exposed, and I watched him gently elevate it to reach the syrinx—two visible lobes and one section hidden just below, adjacent to the heart.

"See one, do one, teach one," he said. "Next one's yours! I really need help full time, if you're interested. Maybe you can take over for me one day and I can retire from devocalizing birds."

I told him I had a packed schedule and a partnership lined up in Carmel, but I could offer one day a week. That was all I could promise.

Back at the emergency clinic that same night, I examined "Dude," a rooster whose throat had been ravaged by a coyote. The family planned to euthanize him, but I offered to try suturing him back together based on the anatomy I'd just learned. They were relieved. Dude was family.

As I placed the final stitches, the receptionist entered the surgery and said, "Dr. Will from Carmel is on the phone. He says it's an emergency."

Dr. Will was the younger veterinarian and my future partner at the Carmel hospital. I feared the senior partner, Dr. Fred, had died unexpectedly.

We've spent the last three months negotiating everything, I thought as I wiped my hands and walked to the phone. Nancy had even enrolled Kelly in kindergarten in Carmel. The price of the practice, the building, the move. Everything!

"Hi Dr. Will," I said, anxious. "Is Dr. Fred okay? The receptionist said it was urgent."

There was a pause. Then Dr. Will said, "Fred's fine. I just had a change of plans and thought you should know. Fred's been asking why I didn't just take over the whole practice myself. Our partnership's been rocky, and my family agrees. Tonight we decided I'll assume ownership and take your deal with Fred. I hope that's okay with you."

I sat in stunned silence. He may as well have told me he'd sold my daughters into slavery in Calcutta and hoped that was okay. What I wanted to say was: *You duplicitous bastard. I've waited patiently for four years. You never*

*once mentioned you might take the practice alone. I
should twist your head off and toss it into Monterey Bay
for shark bait.*

What I said was: "This is not okay. Are you home this
weekend? I'm driving up. I want to hear this from you.
Face to face."

We packed up the girls and drove north under the
pretense of visiting family. I dropped Nancy and the girls
off at her sister's house in the Monterey Bay Area and
drove straight to Dr. Will's house in Carmel. I pounded
on his door.

He opened it cautiously, eyeing me for weapons.
Apparently, I had scared him when I said I was coming
up. His wife hovered nearby, ready to dial 911.

I looked him in the eye and said, "Tell me again what
you told me on the phone."

He stammered, trying to explain. As I listened, the
fury inside me began to settle. One part of me still wanted
to twist his head off. But another part saw clearly: I had
just dodged a bullet. I had seen this man's true character
before I was legally tied to him.

And the truth was, we liked San Clemente. It was warm
and sun-drenched, not foggy and cold like Carmel. I'd
grown up in Berkeley's gray skies and I'd had enough fog
for a lifetime. Dr. Will was also allergic to birds and didn't
want them in the clinic. I was better off without him.

I stood up, extended my hand, and said firmly, "Do not
call me if you get cold feet. I will never go into another
partnership after this experience."

He looked stunned. I turned and left.

Driving back to Nancy's sister's home, part of me felt
shattered. We had spent years pursuing this dream. Yet,

as the miles rolled past and the sky lightened with dawn, another part of me felt liberated. I would now search for my own practice. No partners. No compromises. Just a clear path forward.

Little did I know that my chance encounter with Dr. Svedeen would solve both our problems and mark the beginning of an entirely new chapter.

CHAPTER 13

THE SILVER LINING IN ANOTHER FAILURE

That dream of partnership, and the four years of waiting for it to come to fruition, ended in disaster. But the many trips I took to Monterey in anticipation of that future led me instead to the greatest veterinary epiphany of my life.

It happened at a winery in Paso Robles, a few hours south of Monterey. There, I encountered the healthiest dog I had ever seen in private practice. I had witnessed thousands of lean, muscular animals with lustrous coats in Africa, but back in the US, despite all the "scientifically formulated" diets we recommended, most of the pets I treated looked dull, overweight, or chronically unwell. This dog was different. He was a lean, vibrant Labrador with a coat that shimmered in the sun. He tore across the rural property with effortless energy, tail wagging like a metronome of joy.

While Nancy and her sister sampled wine with a small group, I stayed with the kids and kept watching the Lab. Eventually, I approached the woman pouring the wine, who turned out to be the dog's owner. "What a beautiful dog," I told her. "He's incredibly healthy. Best I've ever seen."

She smiled. "That's Brody," she said. Then she added something that left me speechless: "All the stupid vets told me to send him back to the breeder when he was four months old. They said he had severe hip dysplasia and would be in pain his whole life."

I was stunned. This dazzling, athletic Lab was supposed to be crippled?

At that point, our kids cheerfully outed me as one of the "stupid vets," and the wine server, unfazed, launched into Brody's story. She had been told that if she returned the puppy, she'd receive another one, and Brody would be euthanized. But she refused to give him up. By word of mouth, she learned of a human chiropractor in Monterey who claimed she could heal dogs' hips. Curious and desperate, the owner went to see her.

I expected to hear about some rare alignment technique. Instead, I was floored.

"She told me to throw out the kibble and feed Brody real food," she said. "Just like we eat. Hamburgers, eggs, turkey, fruits and veggies. On Fridays, he gets fish, like a good Catholic," she laughed. "She also recommended vitamin C and a human multivitamin to help with tissue repair."

This went against everything I had learned in vet school. We were taught the only legitimate solution to hip dysplasia was invasive orthopedic surgery—sawing the pelvis into three pieces, realigning it with bone plates, and prescribing anti-inflammatory drugs for life. Yet here stood Brody: healed, drug-free, and overflowing with vitality.

Later that day, I called the chiropractor. Her message was blunt and unforgettable.

"She got rid of the stupid food you stupid vets tell people to feed their pets," she said. "Real food heals. That kibble creates misery, and then you throw drugs at the misery. That's insane."

She wasn't wrong. I remembered the wild dogs, jackals, lions, cheetahs, and leopards I had observed in Africa, India, and Nepal. They were lean, powerful, and vibrant. They ate real food—prey, bones, organs, and I had never heard hip dysplasia mentioned once in wildlife courses.

Back home, I went straight to the San Clemente library and found a book called *Reigning Cats and Dogs: Good Nutrition, Healthy Happy Animals* by Pat McKay. It answered so many of the questions I'd been carrying. The book introduced me to the American Holistic Veterinary Medical Association (AHVMA), which advocated whole food diets and minimal vaccines—radically different from the conventional protocols I'd been taught.

I joined the AHVMA immediately. To my amazement, I found a warm and welcoming community of brilliant, open-minded veterinarians eager to share their knowledge with a rookie. I wrote to a few vets mentioned in the book, asking about Brody's diet. One of them, Dr. Jean Dodds, an expert in immunology and nutrition, personally called me to welcome me. She recommended a whole food supplement called Missing Link to simplify what I'd been trying to replicate with fifteen different vitamins.

Excited but cautious, I tested the diet on five dogs I had scheduled for hip surgeries. There was a months-long waitlist for the one surgeon in Orange County who performed the operation, so I called each family and offered an alternative: real food.

No promises, just a possibility.

To my disbelief and joy, all five dogs fully recovered—within thirty days!—on food alone. No surgery. No drugs. Just whole food and a few supplements.

Since that revelation in 1988, I have preached the miraculous and magical healing power of what I call the "natural diet"—a blend of real animal proteins and plants—to every client who will listen. I consider it the most important health lesson of my career.

Nature is the best medicine, and food is the foundation.

PART THREE:
THE ANIMAL AND
BIRD CLINIC

CHAPTER 14

PEOPLE FOOD FOR PETS

Shortly after my dream job in Monterey Bay went up in flames, Dr. Perry Svedeen in Mission Viejo was facing his own crisis: a failing heart and a stressful practice he could no longer manage alone. In his prime, the Animal and Bird Clinic of Mission Viejo had thrived as an integrative hospital treating birds, exotic animals, and traditional small animal patients. But now, the clinic was open just a few hours a day, caring for species no other veterinarians wanted anything to do with. Tucked between a shoe repair shop and a department store in a modest shopping center, the clinic was aging but still held a spark of its former brilliance.

Dr. Svedeen had asked nearly every veterinarian in Orange County to take over his practice. No one was interested. One of the local Saddleback vets I did relief work for had heard about my failed partnership in Carmel and passed my name along to Dr. Svedeen, who hadn't known I was now jobless. He called me with a hopeful tone, suggesting that I might finally be the right fit. I already had training in avian and exotic medicine and had developed additional expertise in allergies and dermatology—skills the practice needed to survive.

Compared to the betrayal in Monterey, this tiny, time-worn practice felt like a dream come true. My dashed hopes of Northern California were quietly rerouted into the unlikely sanctuary of a small clinic no one else wanted. I promised Dr. Svedeen I would carry on his legacy: his integrative approach to birds, exotics, and small animals alike. On July 9, 1991, we dropped anchor for good at the Animal and Bird Clinic of Mission Viejo.

I knew nothing about running a business, and frankly, I wanted nothing to do with it. That was one of the reasons I had sought a partnership in the first place. But Nancy stepped in with grace and grit. She had studied business in college, run her own company since she was nineteen, and had been teaching high school full time until Kelly was born. I begged her to take on the business side. I promised she'd never have to answer phones or work in the clinic itself.

She set up a remote home office, handling payroll, drug and supply orders, employee benefits, insurance, and a thousand other essential details, all while staying home with the girls. We were centrally located among eight towns, and ours was the only clinic specializing in both holistic care and avian/exotic medicine. The veterinarians I had worked relief shifts for sent all their "unusual" patients, many expected to die, to our clinic. Past clients from the emergency hospital and students from Saddleback College followed me to Mission Viejo. The college's biology department began sending us pre-vet students to gain experience, many of whom became volunteers or part of our growing staff.

I worked six days a week and kept one night open for emergency shifts. I loved every minute. Our team was small, consisting of two young, charming women in their twenties who were trained as both receptionists and technicians. Rather than promoting convenient, heavily marketed industrial pet food, we focused on feeding animals natural, homemade diets based on what they would eat in their native habitats. Forty years ago, this idea was radical. Today, it's foundational to what we now call integrative or functional veterinary medicine.

Back then, it was simply food therapy. And in my experience, it worked a thousand times better than any drug I've prescribed. The animals healed. Their families took notice. And the word began to spread.

Ironically, being an unemployed wildlife ecologist had become the best preparation for life as a holistic "pet vet." I had always dreamed of promoting wellness for wild animals within their ecosystems. Now, I was channeling that same dream into helping pets live longer, healthier lives. I didn't want to be a disease doctor. I wanted to be a wellness doctor.

If we'd focused on profit, we would've pushed heavily processed kibble, vaccinated for everything, and encouraged repeat visits. We might've created a revolving door of sick pets. Instead, we educated families on prevention, on keeping pets out of the clinic with strong immune systems, healthy digestion, and balanced lifestyles. Our goal was for them to visit the vet *less*, not more. That left more time for our patients to thrive, and more time for me to surf.

My understanding of veterinary medicine was soon to be altered even further by the arrival of our next staff member, a charming, elegant, middle-aged English woman named Gail Pope. She wandered into the clinic one morning in 1992 and asked if we needed any help. We did. The phones were ringing off the hook, clients were arriving nonstop, and our small team was stretched thin.

Gail had previously worked for British Airways, escorting celebrities so they didn't have to mingle with the general public. Her husband was a developer assigned to a massive construction project in South Orange County, and Gail was looking for something meaningful to do. Working with animals seemed like a good fit.

We hired her immediately. Her cheerful accent, impeccable manners, and graceful presence made an instant impression. And more importantly, she took to the work with incredible intuition and intelligence.

The front desk of a vet clinic is one of the most emotionally complex, mentally demanding jobs I've ever witnessed. A receptionist might have to answer questions about parrots, pythons, and puppies in the same five-minute span, while checking in an excited family with a new pet, then helping another family say goodbye to a beloved companion. All while processing credit cards, coupons, and ringing phones. It's a maelstrom of emotion and logistics.

Gail handled it all with poise and speed, as if she'd been doing it her entire life. She remembered every patient. She followed their stories. She lit up the waiting room with kindness and care. She was especially fascinated by the dramatic recoveries we saw in cats once they were switched to a natural diet. Formerly crusty, bald, itchy cats would return a month later with thick, glossy coats and bright eyes. Gone were the foul-smelling stools and inflamed skin. In their place: vitality, softness, and relief—for both pet and owner.

Gail was amazed by the feline transformations we witnessed month after month, and truthfully, so was I. Cats were, and still are, the most challenging species when it comes to dietary change, with dogs trailing far behind. Like people, cats become addicted to highly processed food laced with additives that not only damage their health but deepen their dependency.

Dogs, on the other hand, are much less selective. They routinely ingest their own feces and vomit, along with socks, shoes, chocolate candy, marijuana-laced brownies, sofas, tennis balls, and rocks. When introduced to real food, dogs attack it with enthusiasm and rarely crave kibble again. Cats, however, are far more fastidious. Many of them refused to budge from their addiction to dry food, which we jokingly referred to as "kitty crack."

For a time, I tolerated dry food for cats that seemed too addicted to transition. That changed after I read a book that had never been mentioned in veterinary school called *Pottenger's Cats*, by Dr. Francis Pottenger. In the 1940s, Dr. Pottenger had become alarmed by the rising health issues in children consuming processed foods. He turned to cats for answers, conducting a long-term study comparing the effects of processed food versus a raw, whole food diet. His findings were startling: the cats fed whole food thrived for three generations. The processed food group suffered increasingly severe health problems and became unable to reproduce by the third generation, with many dying before the age of ten. Dr. Pottenger feared the same fate would befall children raised on processed food.

He was decades ahead of his time. Today, we know that ultra-processed, sugary food leads to chronic diseases in children like obesity, diabetes, fatty liver, and cancers that were once considered adult conditions.

Since encountering the Wine Country Lab and starting my deep dive into food therapy, I had begun advising cat owners to slowly introduce home-prepared meals that mimicked the makeup of the rodents cats evolved to eat. We recommended a gradual transition: 80 percent meat, eggs, or fish mixed with 20 percent cooked colorful vegetables and a touch of brown rice—while phasing out dry food. For the truly stubborn cases, we used medication for three weeks to help manage the transition. In my experience, 98 percent of cats made the switch.

My first wake-up call about the dangers of dry food came even earlier, while teaching Anatomy and Physiology at Saddleback College. The class was a mix of paramedics-in-training and massage therapists expanding their knowledge. On my first day, I was asked what dog food I recommended. I rattled off the name of a popular brand I'd learned from Doc. A hand shot up belonging to a blonde Swedish masseuse. She looked displeased. "Don't you know there's ethoxyquin in that food? It's poison," she said.

I was embarrassed to admit I'd never once read a pet food label. That night, I started reading them, and what I found was disturbing. Many preservatives used in pet food to ensure a long shelf life are toxic. Cats, especially, suffer the consequences of these industrial diets, just as people do when consuming highly processed foods loaded with sugar and excessive carbohydrates. Like cigarettes, the damage is cumulative. One cigarette doesn't kill you, but ten thousand might. Likewise, pets fed kibble from a young age often suffer chronic diseases years later.

I've seen kibble-fed young dogs and cats die of cancer, and my colleagues in human medicine now routinely treat children for diseases that were once confined to middle-aged adults. The one major change over the last fifty years? Processed food. It overstimulates the brain's reward centers, creating addictions in cats and in kids. The result: a public health crisis, one that veterinarians and pediatricians alike are witnessing firsthand.

Dry cat food contains far more carbohydrates than a natural rodent diet. This unnatural carb load leads to obesity. And these newly minted fat cells don't just sit there. They act as endocrine organs, releasing inflammatory hormones and wreaking havoc on the body. Normally, fat cells produce a hormone called leptin, which signals to the brain that the body is full. But kibble-fed cats become leptin-resistant, flooding their systems with leptin and insulin to no effect. They stay hungry, overeat, and continue storing excess glucose as fat.

It becomes a vicious cycle. The overworked pancreas can't keep up. Insulin receptors become desensitized. Glucose builds up in the bloodstream but can't enter the cells to be burned for energy. The result is fatigue, weight gain, and a condition known as "diabesity." The body begins breaking down muscle tissue to compensate, leading to the production of ketone bodies, which cause nausea and prompt a visit to the vet.

What's extraordinary is that type 2 diabetes in cats, and in people, is not only preventable, but reversible. The answer? A natural diet. If cats ate rodents, they wouldn't get diabetes or fatty liver disease. Since I'm also a rat vet,

I don't encourage my patients to eat each other. Instead, we provide a homemade diet that closely mirrors the nutrient profile of a rodent.

Beyond excessive carbohydrates and toxic preservatives, dry food also damages the microbiome—the diverse community of trillions of beneficial bacteria living in the gastrointestinal tract. Until recently, this vital internal ecosystem was ignored in dogs and cats unless there was diarrhea. In vet school, we studied the cow's microbiome extensively. One of the teaching cows even had a clear porthole sutured into one of its four stomach compartments, allowing us to observe and sample the rich bacterial activity that turns grass into muscle.

The Holistic Veterinary Medical Association has always understood the importance of the microbiome. Now, the rest of the profession is catching up. A healthy microbiome works around the clock to regulate immunity, digestion, mood, and metabolism. When we feed our pets industrial diets, or when we eat the standard American diet, we damage that internal ecosystem and compromise our health.

At a recent veterinary conference, a passionate professor gave a three-hour lecture on feline dermatology. The majority of his time was spent pleading with attendees to stop feeding cats dry food. The preservatives, he argued, were damaging the microbiome and, by extension, the skin. As Doc had told me years earlier, "The skin is a window into the health of the body."

So what does all this have to do with Gail Pope? Everything.

Gail created the greatest living laboratory of whole-food-based feline medicine outside any academic institution. While researchers and staff rotate in and out of universities, Gail built her sanctuary from the ground up. Since the early 1990s, when she walked through our clinic doors, Gail has nurtured her dream, and it continues to thrive.

CHAPTER 15

BRIGHTHAVEN

We had a life expectancy of thirteen years listed on our 1991 wellness handout for cats. Today, our handout lists over twenty years, thanks in large part to Gail and her husband Richard, and their holistic sanctuary called BrightHaven.

Gail had seen cat after cat improve dramatically at our clinic on the homemade, whole food diet. One day she said, "Dr. Doug, I would like to start a sanctuary for old, unwanted cats whose families had to give them up. I want to give these old people a few more years of happiness. I'm going to feed them your diet and treat them as gently and holistically as possible, with love as the main medicine. What do you think?"

"I think that's fantastic," I replied. "And an enormous challenge, but if anyone can do this, it's you, Gail."

I had assumed she would fundraise and use her natural charm, impeccable manners, and sincere grace to rally support. Most of us would have handed over our kids' college funds to Gail without hesitation. But I was wrong. She wasn't fundraising. She started slowly, taking in a few cats from military families facing deployment and elderly people who had passed away, leaving behind young but now unwanted pets. These cats often fell through the cracks of the shelter system and were euthanized or abandoned.

Gail filled this need. She was committed to feeding a fresh, whole food diet to every one of her new residents. Most of the cats she took in had been fed kibble their entire lives. They came with severe dental disease, obesity-induced diabetes (a.k.a. diabesity), and advanced kidney disease.

A few months into her new mission, Gail asked if I would clean some of her "old people's" teeth. I hesitated. Many had failing kidneys, and we were taught in vet school never to anesthetize cats in end-stage kidney disease. "Just humor me and try," she said. "I know they're better after two months on your diet."

Skeptical, I repeated their blood work. As usual, Gail's intuition was spot-on. The values were dramatically improved. I was stunned. We had been taught kidney damage was irreversible, unlike liver disease, where regeneration is possible. But under Gail's care, these old cats were rewriting the textbook.

So we tried it. The first cat, Ringo, went under anesthesia with Sevoflurane, the safest gas available. I extracted diseased teeth and cleaned below the gumline. Extraction is always nerve-racking in older cats because roots can fuse to the jawbone and fracture it during removal. Thankfully, Ringo survived and bounced back, eating better the next day.

As we continued cleaning the teeth of more of Gail's cats, each named after a British rock star, the results were astonishing. Cats that had been written off as terminally ill were thriving. Their kidney values improved. Their energy returned. Our staff became comfortable performing dental procedures on cats well into their twenties. We've never lost a patient and never broken a jaw.

Meanwhile, Gail and Richard expanded their sanctuary. Richard built outdoor cat patios, or "catios," to protect their feline residents from predators like coyotes and hawks. Gail befriended experts in acupuncture, homeopathy, herbal medicine, Chinese medicine, and nutrition. She became a master in immune-stimulating elixirs using New Zealand bovine colostrum and created concoctions so palatable that even the sickest cats would lap them up. We use her formula in our clinic to this day.

Gail began holding Saturday evening homeopathy classes at her ranch, and I eagerly joined. Despite the dozens of cats, her home never smelled like a cat house. Instead, it was bright, clean, and full of life.

When Richard was transferred to Sonoma County, they relocated their sanctuary to Wine Country. One night, he dreamed of the name BrightHaven. It stuck.

Nancy and I still try to visit them whenever we're near UC Davis for continuing education. Their new sanctuary has a custom-built treatment room and the same quiet magic as their original home. Without a doubt, Gail is the finest feline healer I have ever known. As her cats approached the end of their lives, they exhibited signs of peace, purpose, and something beyond what any textbook could ever explain.

CHAPTER 16

BONGO AND THE VIRUS

I'm stuck on a small eco-ship at the port of Punta Arenas, Chile, where local protesters have barricaded us from disembarking and heading to the airport to hike in Patagonia's magnificent Torres del Paine National Park. It's March 16, 2020, and a novel coronavirus has apparently sparked a global pandemic. Every inhabitant of our planet is now affected in some way by the intersection of animals, people, and the microbial life we share, intentionally or not. The moment we find ourselves in is a grim and ironic reminder. This particular coronavirus made the leap from wildlife in China to people, and then to ports around the world.

Viruses are marvels of biochemical engineering. Any awe we might feel for their ingenuity quickly turns to anger once infection sidelines us. They're clever and ruthlessly efficient, hijacking the host's cell nucleus, the brain of the cell, and redirecting it to manufacture viruses instead of the proteins the body needs. They replicate like an out-of-control forest fire, traveling through the bloodstream, lymphatic system, and nerve pathways. The virus triggers the body's defense system, manifesting in coughing, sneezing, diarrhea, and runny noses—all designed to spread viral particles as widely as possible.

A week ago, a cruise ship named the *Vandam* docked here. Passengers seemed fine while in port, but soon after departure, illness broke out in the port and on the ship. One passenger died, and the ship returned, hoping to disembark again, but was denied. They were told to sail away with their sick. Our eco-ship was more fortunate. We were allowed to stay offshore until the Chilean government decided what to do with us. Some people and animals become symptomatic from a virus, while others show no signs. Some never get infected, and others are overtaken. It comes down to the resilience of the individual immune system.

At one o'clock in the morning, I finally fell asleep, viruses heavy on my mind. Protesters had earlier driven us back to the ship with Molotov cocktails when we tried to reach the airport. We were now in quarantine for ten days, floating just offshore.

At three, I woke with a memory. A German shepherd puppy, Bongo, stricken with distemper in the early 1990s. I'd seen the call come in that day, and our receptionist flagged it for isolation. Emma, my technician, took the history. A former Liverpool policewoman, Emma had moved to California with her husband and transitioned into veterinary medicine. Her crisp British accent, bright red hair, and professional grace put every client at ease.

She found me peering under the microscope and gave me the update. "It may take a few minutes to bring you up to speed. Bongo has seen an internist, neurologist, and infectious disease expert. They all told Anna to euthanize him. She found you on a list of holistic vets. She's delightful, very bright. I think she surfs. You'll like them both."

The notes confirmed it: late-stage distemper, confirmed by multiple specialists. I would have recommended euthanasia too. I'd seen many distemper cases while working on the Navajo reservation. "Navajo Retrievers," as we called them, scrappy shepherd mutts, arrived with green discharge from red, inflamed eyes, coughing, snotty noses. The virus often migrated from lungs to the nervous system, triggering signature seizures and the infamous "chewing gum" jaw tremors.

In veterinary school and on the reservation, we were taught that once the chewing-gum seizures begin, the disease is terminal. Treatment was supportive at best. We rarely saw the animals again. Most likely they either succumbed or continued treatment under the guidance of traditional Navajo healers.

I walked into the isolation room and saw Bongo mid-seizure. His guardian, Anna, wore cutoff jeans and a bikini top. She was cradling Bongo's head, trying to keep it from smashing against the floor. I hoped her fingers wouldn't slip into his chattering jaws.

Eventually the seizure passed, and we all exhaled. "I think you know why I'm here," she said. "I'm Anna. This is Bongo." Her German accent reminded me of my months living in Garmisch.

"You a surfer?" I asked.

"Yes! I hear you are too. Wasn't the swell clean and glassy this morning?" she said with a spark in her eyes. We bonded instantly over waves.

She explained how she'd found Bongo in a box marked "Free Puppies" along the Ortega Highway. "He poked his head out and looked right at me. I couldn't leave him."

Now, after spending thousands on specialists, Anna was being told to give up. She refused. "He eats. He wags. He's my best friend. Please try."

Her passion and persistence were palpable. I agreed to try, explaining I had limited experience with neurological distemper, but we'd do no harm and possibly much good. I outlined a plan to stimulate Bongo's antiviral immune system and emphasized avoiding inflammatory foods.

Anna, however, was already well ahead. She'd done hours of research, more than I'd done since vet school, and produced pages of European journal articles. She'd read deeply into the molecular biology of the virus. Her knowledge of viral structure and immune defense was remarkable. This wasn't a last-ditch emotional plea. It was an informed strategy.

We developed a nutrition plan: organic meats, lightly cooked fish, eggs, five-color vegetables like spinach, carrots, sweet potatoes, cabbage, and a few fruits like blueberries. Each food group was chosen for its antiviral, antioxidant, or anti-inflammatory properties. The supplements included cold water fish oils (for neurological inflammation), Missing Link recovery formula (with colostrum, echinacea, medicinal mushrooms, flaxseed, and noni), and vitamin C powder.

It was a lot to manage, but Anna never wavered. Bongo, it turned out, had never been vaccinated, likely due to being abandoned too young to receive adequate immunity from his mother. He was unprotected when he contracted the virus.

Together, we committed to the protocol. Anna never missed a dose. Blood work showed slow but steady progress.

His white blood cell count rose from 3,000 to 12,000 over six months—a strong sign of immune recovery.

As the proverb goes, "It's not the size of the dog in the fight, but the size of the fight in the dog." Bongo had both. And so did Anna. Her love, research, and discipline were heroic.

Decades later, I still remember Bongo as a miracle. His immune system never fully recovered, and he remained vulnerable to illness if he went off the supplements and diet. But thanks to Anna's tireless care, he lived. And he lived well.

As I floated off the coast of Chile, thinking about COVID and distemper, immune systems and Molotov cocktails, I reminded myself and my fellow passengers that our best protection has always been within. Sleep, sunshine, breath, whole foods, and love. That's how we heal.

CHAPTER 17

THE FATE OF NATE

Some viruses are clever, and some are just plain stupid. And it's the stupid ones that wreak havoc and kill quickly. A virus's goal is simple: hijack a host cell, turn it into a virus-making machine, and spread. A clever virus does this without killing the host too quickly, preserving its ride. A stupid virus kills its host, dooming itself in the process. The coronavirus keeping me quarantined off the Chilean coast is clever. It spreads stealthily, often symptomless at first, but later proved fatal for thousands. It's faster, more contagious, and more lethal than the seasonal flu.

My most unforgettable, and heartbreaking, experience with a virus came about a year after we opened our clinic. A six-month-old miniature pinscher was brought in for hair loss by his owner Tim, a mild-mannered computer wizard who also bred Burmese pythons. I usually saw Tim when his snakes had pneumonia, but this visit was different. The puppy had patchy hair loss across his tiny frame. I did a skin scraping and viewed the slide under the microscope. It was crawling with Demodex mites, microscopic parasites shaped like translucent cigars. "Oh no," said Tim when I told him. "I can't breed a dog with Demodex. I'll have to euthanize him."

The puppy, adorable and full of bounce, licked me joyfully. "Would you be okay if I treated him and found him a home?" I asked. Tim was visibly relieved. "Only if you keep him, Dr. Coward."

We named him Nate, after basketball legend Nate "Tiny" Archibald, and started him on the homemade natural diet of organic meats, vegetables, Missing Link supplement, fish oil, and colostrum. His fur returned, glossy and full, and after six weeks the mites were gone without a single medicated dip. His vitality exploded. He bounced around like a dik-dik, miniature gazelles we saw in Kenya.

But Nate wasn't perfect. He had two issues: he liked to mark every inch of our carpet with his urine, and he had overactive anal glands that he often released while curled up on someone's lap. His laps of choice were frequent and uninvited. Despite his faults, Nate had thousands of endearing qualities. He especially adored Shawn, sleeping every night under her covers, never marking that sacred space.

Nate was nine when it struck. The night before, we had taken our usual late-night walk—our ritual of breathing the sea air, watching stars above the Pacific, checking surf and tides. Nate thought the whole walk was for him. That morning I paddled out for Dawn Patrol at San Onofre with my neighbor Dr. Randy. The waves were clean and glassy, the sun warmed our backs, and the water shimmered in kaleidoscopic blues and greens. We caught our quota, our immune systems rejoicing from the flood of natural neurotransmitters and happy hormones.

I returned home to a call from Sherri, our early-morning tech: two emergencies were waiting in the parking lot. I wasn't due at the clinic until 8:30 a.m., but I raced in. We stabilized a convulsing African gray parrot with low calcium from egg-laying and began treating a six-month-old Lab, Beau, who had developed severe vomiting and diarrhea overnight. He was up to date on vaccines, so Parvo seemed unlikely. We placed an IV, drew samples, and started fluids, vitamin C, B complex, and glucose.

Then Sarah, our receptionist, called back to the treatment area: "Shawn's on the phone. It's an emergency!"

My stomach dropped. "Dad, come home. Nate's sick. He won't eat or move." I rushed home. Shawn met me, stricken. I entered her room and found Nate, limp, barely breathing. "He woke me up," Shawn said through tears. "He looked right at me, then got sick on the pillow. I cleaned it, and when I came back, he was worse. It all happened in an hour."

I hugged her, scooped up Nate, and sped to the clinic. I broke every traffic law. The staff saw my face. No one had ever seen me like that. We acted fast: IV fluids, antibiotics, immune stimulants, a warming pad. Juan, our top tech, drew blood from Nate's collapsing veins. Minutes later, the results were in: a white blood cell count of 1,000, lower than anything I'd seen. Beau's count? 1,500. Also critically low.

White cells are the immune system's military. These boys had been ambushed.

We needed plasma immediately. We called All-Care Animal Referral Center. "Sorry," said Sherri, "they're out. Huge demand this morning. First time ever."

At eleven o'clock, Nate perked up. Nancy had called, and it was like he heard her. But moments later, his eyes glazed. He seized violently. Blood trickled from his nose. He took one last breath. I gave epinephrine, intubated him, did CPR. Nothing. I wrapped him in a towel and collapsed outside in the lunch area, holding him in my lap. The tears flowed. I couldn't stop them. No one interrupted me until eventually, I felt a soft tap on my arm. It was Nancy, Shawn, and Kelly. "It's okay, Dad," Kelly said. "We know you tried."

They had never seen me in such a speechless, tearful state. I could say nothing except to sob, "I'm so sorry," and hung my head in utter shame. I felt more tender pats, but I couldn't lift my head. *How did I let this happen?* That's my job, to heal and help animals recover, and I failed my own family.

Shawn leaned into Nancy. We embraced. I could only whisper again, "I'm sorry."

We held a small wake for Nate. Buried him under honeysuckle to attract hummingbirds, which were his favorite. I surfed the next morning. The rising sun, the perfect waves, and the grace of nature helped me breathe again. I brought donuts to the clinic as a peace offering for our staff, because I couldn't face them empty-handed.

Richard Mackey, my vet school friend and clinic partner, took over Beau's care. But by morning, he too had passed after being sent to the ER with worsening symptoms. They diagnosed DIC: Disseminated Intravascular Coagulation. Our professor called it "Death Is Coming." Beau had bled out from the inside.

The next morning, Scott Penny brought in Hulk, his Yorkie. "He vomited once," he said, frantic. "My sister's a vet in LA. She says thirty-five dogs died yesterday from a new virus. Please help him."

We ran blood work—low-normal white count—but all else looked good. I didn't mention Nate or Beau. Scott's sister later called, thanking me. "It's horrible in LA," she said. "Please pray for him." We did. Hulk recovered.

Unlike the stealthy coronavirus spreading across the globe, the virus that took Nate and Beau was brutally fast. It hit hard, killed quickly, and burned itself out in two weeks. As I write this, I don't know what the future holds with this pandemic. But as of March 20, 2020, I'm still afloat off Punta Arenas, Chile, with time to remember Bongo, Beau, and Nate—and honor their stories.

CHAPTER 18

LESSONS ON BIRD HEALING FROM A WEDDING

It continues to amaze me how chance encounters dramatically change the way I practice. Doc gave me great advice early on: attend continuing education meetings, and keep your ears open during coffee breaks and happy hours. He was adamant that he personally treated all sick birds. He believed families couldn't properly medicate them at home, and they would die without the supportive care only a hospital could provide. By keeping birds in his avian hospital, tube feeding anorexic patients, giving subcutaneous fluids with vitamins, and administering injectable antibiotics, Doc believed he gave them the best chance at survival. Since he was the only vet I knew with three decades of avian medicine experience, I listened and learned.

When we took over for Dr. Svedeen, who was as skilled and experienced in avian medicine as Doc, and shared a similar treatment philosophy, I continued practicing as I'd been taught. I hospitalized every sick bird and followed the blueprint passed down to me.

In 1995, Melissa came in on a Tuesday with her very sick cockatiel, Sydney. Melissa, in her late twenties, always brought Sydney in for annual checkups and wing trims.

She took impeccable care of her bird. Cockatiels are fabulous little parrots, vocal, social, and affectionate. I saw thousands living free in Australia. In the wild, if one member of a flock shows weakness, the others will mob and kill the sick bird to avoid attracting predators. As pets, cockatiels are charming and engaging, but a critically ill cockatiel is unrecognizable: puffed feathers, closed eyes, lethargy, and silence. They're often a heartbeat from death by the time they show symptoms.

Our technician Catherine checked Melissa and Sydney in while I finished up with another patient. Catherine was one of our best. She'd started working with us at fourteen and, after a stint in human health care, returned to veterinary medicine, saying, "People are mean. Animals are lovely." Her return was a blessing.

"Dr. C, this is not good," she said. "Sydney is 78 grams, has a prominent keel bone, pasted vent, and sinus discharge. Melissa is getting married Saturday in Napa and wants Sydney in the wedding. You'll need to work a miracle."

I walked into the room and found Melissa, normally cheerful, in tears. "I don't know what happened," she cried. "She didn't sing this morning. She won't eat. Her fanny is all dirty, but it's always clean."

I gently wrapped Sydney in a towel and misted her with Bach's Rescue Remedy, a calming floral essence. Her conjunctiva were red. Fluid oozed from her nares. Her heart raced over 200 beats per minute. Although her lungs were still clear, her weight loss indicated weeks of illness. She had no energy to resist being weighed.

Sydney's feathers were in good shape, no stress lines, which show up in birds malnourished on seed diets. She'd been eating chopped vegetables, fruit, and organic pellets from Dr. Greg Harrison. But now her vent was caked with green diarrhea. She was in critical condition.

I proposed a treatment plan: nebulizer therapy with oxygen and antibiotics, tube feeding with EmerAid slurry, subcutaneous fluids with vitamins, and an eventual blood panel to assess her immune system and organ function once she stabilized. But Melissa shook her head.

"You can't keep her, Dr. Coward. We're driving to Napa this afternoon. She'll be fine. She has to be there. I'll pray, and you can do what you can in thirty minutes."

I hesitated. I'd never sent a cockatiel this sick out of the clinic. "I really think you should leave her here," I said gently. "She needs intensive care."

"She'll be fine," Melissa insisted. "She wants to be in the wedding."

We did what we could. We gave her ten minutes in the nebulizer, fed her a warm slurry through a crop tube, administered fluids and a shot of Enrofloxacin. We sent Melissa with antibiotic nose drops, immune-boosting herbs, and a vial of EmerAid. I reminded her to keep the car and hotel room warm.

"Don't worry," she said. "Sydney will be warm. And please pray for her." I gave her a hug and wished her the perfect wedding day.

A week passed. Then, on a busy Saturday morning, Catherine shouted, "It's Melissa, and she sounds happy!"

I picked up the phone, unsure of what to expect. I heard a cockatiel chirping. Then Melissa's voice: "Sydney's back to normal! She's going to be on my shoulder when I walk down the aisle!"

"Just don't forget to cover your dress," I laughed. "Green spots every twenty minutes!"

"I told you she'd be fine. Thanks for praying, and for listening," she said.

I was stunned. I'd given Sydney a 1 percent chance. But Melissa believed in her. Years later, I'd come to understand the biological power of love and intention. Just like the Wine Dog changed how I saw nutrition, Sydney and Melissa forever changed how I saw healing.

CHAPTER 19

PLEAS FROM ALEX THE PARROT

Three weeks later, I got another surprise. I was making the same long ride up the Central Valley to UC Davis, just thirty miles south of Melissa's Napa wedding, headed to the annual avian and exotic animal conference at the veterinary school. Dr. Irene Pepperberg was speaking about her experience training Alex, the legendary African gray parrot. I had already read her fascinating book and was eager to hear her in person.

Having lived with parrots since 1975, I knew them to be sentient, cognitive, affectionate, and often mischievous. They could also be irritable, vindictive, and temperamental during breeding season. Our male cockatoo, George, adored Nancy, who had hand-raised him in Melbourne during the disco era. George resented me and caused endless mischief. He'd laugh when we missed basketball shots in our yard. He'd wolf-whistle at college coeds jogging by, then duck behind the bushes while I got the finger. George loved to dance, especially when we had company. Nancy would cue him, and he'd perform like a born entertainer.

Parrots are far less common in the US than in Australia, and most Americans still associate "bird brain" with stupidity. But Dr. Pepperberg's thirty years of research told a different story. She bought Alex from a pet store at one year old, naming him for the Avian Language Experiment. Scientists had long believed that only large primate brains could manage the complexities of language and cognition. Bird brains were thought capable only of mimicry.

Alex shattered that myth. He could learn, count, identify objects, and even ask questions, something no nonhuman had done. When he looked in a mirror and asked, "What color?" he was told "gray." He learned and remembered. He identified over fifty objects and developed a vocabulary of one hundred words. In one famous moment, when hospitalized for a fungal infection, Alex called out, "Don't leave me here!" Dr. Pepperberg took him home against veterinary advice and nursed him back to health with outpatient visits for treatment.

After recounting this, she paused, looked at the audience, and said, "You need to reconsider hospitalizing parrots. Alex told me not to leave him, so I didn't. Your clinics are stressful. Please listen to your patients and their families. There's no place like home for healing."

In that moment, I thought of Sydney. Melissa had known what her bird needed. I had almost overridden that instinct.

I began asking parrot owners if they could medicate their birds at home. Some parrots leap out of their cages and accept oral medication willingly. Others? Not so much. I was especially wary of suggesting families give pectoral injections—those should only be handled by trained staff. But many were happy to bring birds in for outpatient treatments, then return home for recovery.

To my surprise and delight, birds I'd given no chance of survival began to recover at home, in the arms of their loving families. We expanded this approach to reptiles, dogs, and cats. They, too, recovered faster when surrounded by love. I hadn't yet applied this lesson to surgical patients, but I would very soon.

CHAPTER 20

SOPHIE AND STEPHANIE'S CHOICE

I received another reminder that healing often defies conventional wisdom. This next veterinarian epiphany began with a phone call from my neighbor Marty.

"Hi Doug, this is Marty. How was the surf this morning? Did you go out?" he asked.

"Yes, I did Dawn Patrol," I replied. "Just a few guys out, glassy and five feet. Did you make it out?"

Marty had gone later that morning at eight thirty in the morning and said it was great. Then he added, "Would you be able to have a look at Sophie? Something's wrong. She won't get out of her bed. She tries but looks like she's drunk and just staggers. We'd all be grateful if you have time to come by."

Sophie was their German shorthaired pointer, a familiar sight jogging with Marty's German wife, Stephanie. I'd seen them for years while surfing at San Onofre, so I estimated Sophie was well over ten years old.

Marty's description over the phone immediately suggested Geriatric Vestibular Syndrome, also known as "Old Dog Stroke." It's often idiopathic, which means it arises spontaneously or for reasons we don't yet understand. The inner ear's vestibular system controls balance, so any disturbance makes an animal appear drunk. Most dogs recover in a few weeks. Confident in that diagnosis, I rode my bike two blocks to Marty's house.

Their son greeted me anxiously and led me to the laundry room where Sophie lay on a blanket. But the moment I saw her, I knew I'd been wrong. Her eyes weren't darting side-to-side. And when I lifted her lip, I saw white gums, an ominous sign of internal bleeding.

I checked her femoral pulse: rapid and weak. She was losing blood. When I palpated her abdomen, I felt a large mass near her spleen. Most likely, it was a hemangiosarcoma—a tumor of blood vessels that can rupture, causing life-threatening internal hemorrhage. There was no blood from her mouth or rectum. She was bleeding into her abdomen.

Stephanie had just arrived. I quickly explained what was likely happening and what we needed to do: X-rays, blood work, emergency surgery. Stephanie froze.

"Please, Doug, do something now, but no surgery. I have to fly to Germany in an hour. My mother is ill. I can't bear to be on a plane not knowing what's happening to Sophie in surgery. Please, anything but surgery," she pleaded. "And she has to stay in our home. I want her with Marty and the boys."

Marty said nothing, just nodded. He trusted her intuition.

This was new territory for me. I'd never treated a bleeding splenic tumor without surgery.

But I listened.

"There's an herbal remedy called Yunnan Baiyao," I said. "It's been used for over a hundred years in China. During the Vietnam War, our medics noticed gravely injured North Vietnamese soldiers who hadn't bled out because they had taken this herb. We've used it with good results before and after surgery to reduce bleeding."

I then asked what Sophie ate. "Kibble," Stephanie said.

I explained how processed food could worsen inflammation because kibble is full of toxic activated glycation end products, or AGEs, and preservatives which damage the microbiome, trigger mutations and tumor growth.

I offered an alternative:

"Start slowly. Use ground turkey, lightly cooked, and mix in colorful cooked vegetables like broccoli, kale, carrots, sweet potatoes, and a bit of brown rice."

"That's how we fed dogs back in Germany," she said. "Whatever we ate, they ate. No one used kibble."

"Perfect," I replied. "Next, we'll add fish oils to decrease inflammation and inhibit blood supply to tumors. Then there's Noni, a fruit used for centuries in Polynesia for its anticancer and pain-relieving properties. And a supplement called Onco Support, which stimulates cancer-killing cells. It contains mushrooms, green tea extract, spirulina, milk thistle, amino acids, and probiotics all to help the immune system, detoxify the liver, and support gut health."

It was a lot to absorb, especially for someone like Marty, a brilliant electrical engineer but new to holistic pet care. I typed out everything and pedaled home, then drove to the clinic to gather the supplies. I also collected referrals to integrative oncology experts like Dr. Greg Ogilvie for chemotherapy, radiation treatment, and high-tech immunotherapy.

When I returned, I was relieved to find Sophie still alive. We gave her two Yunnan Baiyao capsules, and I showed Marty how to prepare the whole food diet. I encouraged him to hand-feed her if needed. By day five, Sophie was eating on her own.

After three weeks, she began to run again. She passed peacefully at home six months later, at age thirteen and a half, after defying all expectations.

I had never considered "hospice care" for a bleeding splenic tumor. Stephanie's intuition challenged my training and changed my thinking. Once again, a woman's instinct and a family's love rewrote the medical script and added another chapter to the way I practice veterinary medicine.

CHAPTER 21

HAMSTER WHISPERER WRITES A BESTSELLER

When we finally settled into the new state-of-the-art clinic Nancy built across from Mission Viejo High School, I began seeing people and pets repeatedly over the years for the first time in my veterinary career. I started asking about the other end of the leash, and I loved what I learned. That part of the practice became just as fascinating as the medicine. People are so different in how they acquire and name their pets. Because we treat such a diverse crew of animals, we attract an equally eclectic mix of humans. There are snake people, cat people, bird lovers, rabbit rescuers, dog devotees, and herp enthusiasts. Then there are the blends: people who adore dogs and rats but hate cats. Some, like me, love them all.

The reception room could sometimes feel like a social experiment: a quiet computer engineer cradling a bunny sits next to a tattooed millennial with a twelve-foot Burmese python draped around their shoulders, eyeing that bunny like an appetizer.

In the mid-1990s, a thoroughly entertaining young woman named Stacey arrived with the most animals anyone had ever brought in at once: thirty Syrian hamsters. Stacey looked like a character out of a Swiss children's book, with her blonde pigtails and calm confidence. I introduced myself as she calmly injected one of her hamsters.

"I have to give him pain meds," she said casually.

I'd never seen a client do that in the exam room unless we were teaching them how to give insulin. She handed me a few pages of handwritten notes describing symptoms and treatments. Each hamster had a name. They all looked identical to me.

"Are they OK to handle?" I asked hesitantly. Syrian hamsters were notorious for biting. My fingers had the scars to prove it.

"Yes, of course," Stacey smiled, handing me one.

To my surprise, they were all friendly. Stacey had hand-raised them and bred them herself. Only a few needed medication. I asked if she was a medical doctor or a zoologist.

"I'm a research associate at Caltech," she replied. "I work with all kinds of animals. But hamster vets are impossible to find. I had to drive over an hour to get here."

Stacey's empathy and commitment to these tiny, temperamental creatures was astonishing. She was clearly a gifted animal whisperer. Over the years, I saw Stacey occasionally for surgeries to remove hamster tumors. She'd always ask more about me, and I'd do the same. She told me she'd been a child actress and a biology major at Occidental College. She loved working at Caltech with all the "weird geniuses."

About a decade after we first met, Stacey asked to speak in private. I ushered her into an exam room.

"Would you treat my barn owl in an emergency and not tell anyone?" she asked.

"Of course," I said. "I worked with barn owls at Davis. They're my favorite."

Stacey explained that a Caltech professor had given her a four-day-old owlet with a broken wing. He believed Stacey's empathy and observational skills could reveal insights about barn owl behavior that were impossible to glean from lab studies. "When I saw him, it was love at first sight. It was Valentine's Day," she said. "I named him Wesley."

I assumed she'd only had him a few months because raising owlets is messy and demanding. "Wesley is seventeen," she said.

"Months?"

"Years."

I was stunned. She'd fed him over twenty thousand mice and lost relationships over Wesley's messy, sometimes amorous behaviors. "I gave him my word," she said. "He's my life."

She asked if I could train my staff to use a code—"It's Wesley"—so no one would say the word "owl" in front of clients. Not everyone approved of her keeping a wild owl in captivity.

"No problem," I said. I told the team Wesley could come any time, and I'd stay late if needed.

Years passed. One night, Sarah, our gregarious receptionist, told me, "Stacey called. She said, 'It's Wesley.' She's on her way."

Sarah stayed to help, sensing this wasn't a normal after-hours visit. Stacey arrived looking distraught. "Wesley collapsed," she said. He was emaciated. I laid him gently on a warm towel while Stacey whispered her love. Sarah wrapped her arms around her.

I listened to Wesley's heart with my pediatric stethoscope. It was dangerously slow. As I focused, it stopped.

"Stacey," I said gently. "His heart just stopped."

We tried everything—oxygen, drugs, CPR. Nothing worked. Wesley was gone.

Between sobs, Stacey asked for a necropsy. I performed it immediately. His liver was shrunken and nodular, riddled with cancer. I returned to tell her.

"You kept him alive longer than anyone else could have," I said. "You're a miracle worker."

Later that night, I shed tears for both of them.

Weeks later, Stacey called. Her voice was bright. "I wrote a story about Wesley. You're in it. Can I use your name?"

"Sure," I said. "Though no one will believe there's a vet named Coward."

She laughed. I thought she'd write a pamphlet for friends. But months later, she returned with a thick book featuring essays by Jane Goodall and others. And a chapter on Wesley.

"You did it!" I said. "I'm so proud of you."

A year later, she brought me a copy of her own book: *Wesley the Owl: The Remarkable Love Story of an Owl and His Girl*, by Stacey O'Brien. She signed it with a personal note.

I loved the book and so did the rest of the country. It became a national bestseller. Wherever I go, checking bookstores in New York, San Francisco, and San Diego, her book is always there. Old classmates have written, saying they read the story with a vet named Coward and wondered if it could possibly be me.

It was.

The longer I practiced, the more fascinated I became by the human-animal bond, a term never mentioned when I was in vet school. We animal lovers know what it means without needing a definition. Stacey's relationship with a wild barn owl, known for being solitary and shy, was as deep as any golden retriever's loyalty to their human.

The human-animal bond isn't hardwired into everyone. Some people just don't get it. They say, "They smell, they shed, they poop."

But animal lovers hardly notice. We see only the gifts they bring.

And some, like Stacey and Wesley, live a love story for the ages.

CHAPTER 22

THE ENDEARING BOND OF CORKY AND RICH

With each new patient I met, I was always curious about the nature and depth of the bond they shared with their human. It was often unpredictable. I completely misjudged the bond Rich Myers would form with his dachshund, Corky.

Rich was a delightful bon vivant. He'd dated Nancy's best friend in college, along with, apparently, half the other coeds. All were hopelessly smitten with Rich, who remained a confirmed and content bachelor. I had met him a few times at family and work gatherings, as his nephew, Dr. Greg Myers, was one of our beloved staff veterinarians. Rich and I hit it off over our shared love of surf culture and fly fishing. We saw more of him after he moved to nearby Dana Point.

Eventually, a girl did steal Rich's heart. She was a wire-haired dachshund named Corky. I assumed carefree Rich would provide the basics for Corky, but no deeper commitment. I couldn't have been more wrong.

I first saw Corky and Rich when Dr. Greg was on vacation. Normally, Rich would see his nephew, and they'd catch up on family news. The staff loved Rich. He was about ten years older than me, still handsome and fit, with a perpetually warm grin and a few movie credits from his time in Hawaii during the late 1960s.

Catherine checked Rich and Corky into the exam room and came out visibly concerned. "Rich said Corky stopped eating and started vomiting this morning. She's drinking and peeing a lot. He's worried, and so am I," she said.

I entered the room. "DUUUH-ug!" Rich beamed, greeting me with his signature drawl. "How was the surf this morning?"

"Pretty perfect," I replied, rubbing the bump on my temple. "Until I pearled and my board smacked me in the head. My buddies were thoroughly entertained."

Corky looked up at me with soulful, gentle brown eyes. Always sweet, always cooperative, she looked genuinely unwell.

"She loves to eat," Rich said. "That's why I'm worried."

Mentally, I ran through the causes of increased thirst and urination, which could be urinary tract infections, kidney disease, and in unspayed females, the possibility of pyometra: a severe uterine infection. "Has Corky been spayed?" I asked.

Rich paused. "I don't think so. Her original owner considered breeding her but never went through with it."

We kept Corky for testing, hoping for a simple bladder infection. But what we found was far more serious: sky-high blood sugar, signs of kidney stress, and a uterus filled with pus. Corky had both diabetic ketoacidosis and pyometra, two life-threatening emergencies.

Normally, pyometra requires immediate surgery. But Corky's diabetes had to be stabilized first, or she'd die under anesthesia. We started her on IV fluids, short-acting insulin, and close monitoring.

The next day I was in San Diego at one of Kelly's surf contests when Corky underwent the risky surgery by Rich's nephew, Dr. Greg, to remove her swollen and infected uterus before it burst. Corky survived, but she'd need lifelong insulin injections, twice per day. I called Rich, fully expecting he might opt to say goodbye. After all, he had a spontaneous, travel-heavy lifestyle, and this was the most homework I'd given for a patient.

Instead, Rich said, "I know you'll do your best, and I'll do mine."

He threw himself into Corky's care: preparing home-made food, giving insulin twice daily, and boosting her immunity. Later, when Corky developed malignant mammary tumors, common in unspayed females, Dr. Greg removed them, and pathology gave her less than a year to live. Rich called me in distress.

"Greg says she's got a year, maybe less. Do you have one of your crazy diets to help?"

His friends suggested pizza, ice cream, and beer for her last days. Rich chose broccoli and turkey instead.

He embraced our anticancer, antidiabetic diet: organic meats and vegetables, blended and lightly cooked, with supplements like fish oil, colostrum, medicinal mushrooms, Missing Link and Onco Support. We traded beer for green tea with organic honey. Corky thrived.

Then came autoimmune hypothyroidism and dry eye. We added thyroid medication and cyclosporine drops to the already intensive "Corky care" protocol. Rich never once complained.

Through it all—pollen allergies, hormone imbalances, surgeries, and daily injections—Rich remained devoted. Corky, now a beautiful and loving senior citizen of fourteen years, is still with us. I never would have believed the Porsche-driving, road-tripping bachelor would become such a dedicated caretaker with an unbreakable bond.

I was wrong again. And I've never been happier to be wrong.

CHAPTER 23

BISCUIT THE VERY YELLOW LAB

Two patients arrived nearly simultaneously, both from San Clemente, with conditions that were unprecedented and frightening. Biscuit came first, accompanied by her devoted mom, Cynthia Cooper. Catherine, an RN and veterinary technician, briefed me. "Cynthia is really worried. Biscuit's depressed, and you know how happy she normally is. She won't wag her tail or eat. She just lies around all day."

Cynthia was one of the kindest, most humble and intelligent animal lovers I'd ever met. She and her husband Craig, her high school sweetheart, were instrumental in founding the San Clemente animal shelter. Cynthia, a whiz with numbers, managed the shelter's finances; Craig, a financial adviser, brought his own expertise to the cause.

Biscuit, a sweet yellow Lab, was normally a nonstop tail-wagger and affection machine. Unfortunately, she had drawn a tough genetic hand: chronic allergies, arthritis, and epilepsy. We'd been treating her conventionally, with some integrative support for her joints.

When I walked into the exam room, I was stunned. Biscuit wasn't just yellow-furred. She was yellow everywhere! Her gums, eyes, even her skin. Cynthia, usually radiant, was in tears.

"I don't know what happened, Dr. Doug. She was fine two days ago, and now she won't move or eat."

Biscuit was indeed lifeless. Her jaundice was the worst I'd ever seen. There were several potential causes. Either her red blood cells were breaking down faster than her liver could process them (hemolysis), or her liver was failing to clear bilirubin, a by-product from red blood cell breakdown. Either way, something was seriously wrong.

"We'll run some blood tests and have answers in about an hour," I told Cynthia.

"Do you think she can recover?" she asked.

"The liver is a forgiving organ," I said gently. "As long as this isn't cancer, there's hope. But I won't lie. This is serious."

Biscuit was carefully moved to the treatment area. Juan and Rosa drew blood and placed an IV catheter. Her serum, normally clear, was bright yellow. Thirty minutes later, the blood work came back. The numbers were terrifying.

Her bilirubin was over 20 (normal is under 3.6). Protein levels were dangerously low. She had ascites, or fluid in the abdomen, a result of the liver failing to make albumin. Her immune-supporting globulin levels were also critically low. X-rays and ultrasound confirmed the fluid buildup but showed no tumors or abscesses. The entire liver appeared damaged.

We began aggressive treatment: IV fluids enriched with vitamins B and C, detoxifying herbs like milk thistle and dandelion, and amino acids to help her rebuild essential proteins. We contacted Hemopet, Dr. Jean Dodds's nonprofit blood bank, and retrieved fresh frozen plasma to transfuse her with the antibodies, clotting proteins, and nutrients her own liver could no longer produce.

Still, we didn't know why her liver had failed. A biopsy was necessary, but her condition made it too risky. Over the next days, Biscuit barely improved. We fed her nutrient-dense meatballs by hand made of white fish, spinach, sweet potato, and supplements. She would reluctantly swallow them.

Meanwhile, I was days away from flying to France to watch my daughter Kelly compete in the women's world longboard surfing championships. The year before, after competing in Costa Rica, Kelly had qualified for the world stage in Biarritz. She was elated. "You should be here, Dad! They treat us like NBA All-Stars!" she'd said. I'd promised her I would come the next year. Nancy, too, had travel dreams: a visit to Eastern Europe, including Prague and Budapest, with friends we knew from San Clemente.

But as our departure approached, Biscuit's condition weighed heavily on me. Her protein levels dropped again and she needed another transfusion. The results of a fine needle aspirate were inconclusive. To get a definitive answer, we needed a surgical biopsy.

Cynthia, normally soft-spoken, was firm. "No anesthesia. No surgery. I just don't feel right about it."

I couldn't argue. Her intuition had always been on point. On the morning of our flight, I called the clinic from the car. Biscuit was receiving another transfusion. I hung up, heart heavy, uncertain if I'd ever see her again.

I worried about Biscuit during the flight to Prague. The next morning, we were up at dawn, walking the cobblestone streets and crossing the Charles Bridge, the historic heart of Czech spirit. I had read in the *Lonely Planet* guide that pilgrims were granted one prayer wish in a lifetime if they rubbed the plaque beneath the statue of St. John of Nepomuk. I knew my wish.

Nancy, unaware of the legend, asked what I was doing. "I'm using up my one and only prayer," I told her. She nodded, rubbed the plaque herself, and made her own wish.

From Prague, we traveled to Biarritz. The women's surf championships were even more magical than Kelly had described with giant banners, warm welcomes, gourmet food, espresso, and a lively festival atmosphere. But my thoughts kept drifting back to Biscuit.

When we returned, I learned Biscuit was home, eating, wagging her tail, and nearly back to normal. I called Cynthia. Her voice was bright.

"Oh, Dr. Doug, I'm so sorry. I had a meltdown. Biscuit got so much worse while you were gone. I thought it was the end. But the next day she turned a corner—it was a miracle! She's been getting better every day."

I did the calendar math. Biscuit's miraculous rebound began right after I rubbed that plaque in Prague.

"Let's recheck her liver tests in three weeks," I said. "And I'll tell you a little story about Prague."

Biscuit's blood work showed a complete recovery. I finally discovered the cause: iatrogenic disease, combined with a genetic mutation found in some Labs. I learned about iatrogenic disease in vet school when a visiting cowboy professor from Washington State said, "God cures eighty percent of your patients. Ten percent get better from your help, and ten percent get worse from your efforts. Don't take too much credit when they heal and don't slit your wrists when you make them worse. The fancy name for vets making our patients worse is iatrogenic."

Biscuit was initially damaged by my good intentions. We'd been treating her skin yeast with ketoconazole and her seizures with phenobarbital, two drugs requiring healthy liver detoxification. But Biscuit, like some herding breeds and a subset of Labs, had a mutation that impaired her ability to clear certain medications.

When those drugs piled up in her system, her liver couldn't cope. It nearly shut down.

Now I treat skin yeast and seizures with herbs, food therapy, and supplements. I took a week-long course in Chinese medicine and learned about customizing herbal treatments based on timing and patterns, and I lean on that insight far more than I once did.

Phenobarbital is now my last resort. Biscuit taught me well.

She recovered fully and lived a happy, healthy life without medications. And I like to think a prayer from a faraway bridge played a part in saving her life.

CHAPTER 24

BRIX: ANOTHER LAST-CHANCE PUPPY

B rix is one dog I can confidently say I helped, or rather that a team of veterinary holistic experts helped.

She came into my life not long after leaping into the hearts of Carol and David Westendorf, fellow San Clemente residents who lived just a few blocks from me. When Catherine finished checking Brix in, she came over to my desk, sat down, and said, "I hope you have lots of time. This history is long."

Brix was a four-month-old Portuguese water dog who had already seen every specialist in Orange County. According to the neurologist, she'd had distemper as a puppy that likely damaged her hypothalamus—the part of the brain that controls appetite. "She won't eat," Catherine said. "That's why she's here. Your surfing buddy RB is their neighbor. He told them you might have a holistic approach. I really hope we can help. Brix is so sweet." She added, "Oh, and her vitals are perfect: heart rate, respiration, temperature. She looks totally normal."

I didn't actually know what a normal Portuguese water dog looked like. But when I walked into the exam room and saw Brix, she took my breath away. She looked like a poodle version of a class clown with panache. Curly black fur with a white chin patch, bright angel eyes full of personality, and a charm that radiated from her little twenty-pound body.

Her owner, Caroline, looked like she had stepped off an Olympic beach volleyball court. She was tall, athletic, and always smiling. "Hi, Dr. Coward. Brix is here for you to fix," she said warmly, while stroking Brix gently.

"Brix is so much smaller than her sisters," she said. "We've tried everything. Every specialist gave up and told us to get another puppy. But I love her so much. I'll try anything."

Catherine handed me a stack of specialist reports. The conclusions were grim: either surgically implant a permanent feeding tube or euthanize her.

Brix was thin but otherwise normal. "I can leave her with you if you think that's best," Caroline offered. I agreed. We already had another patient, Biscuit, being hand-fed in the hospital, so we placed Brix next to her and added a few extra "Biscuit Balls" to try coaxing her to eat.

After Caroline kissed Brix goodbye, I reviewed the records. Everyone was stumped. Her labs, x-rays, ultrasound—all normal. She'd had a nonlethal case of distemper, but if left untreated, it could still prove fatal.

In challenging, head-scratching cases like this, I often reached out to my go-to integrative expert: Dr. Jean Dodds. Dr. Dodds may be the busiest veterinary specialist on the planet. She's conducted pioneering research in vaccines, food sensitivities, endocrine disorders. You name it. She also founded Hemopet, the nonprofit blood bank that had helped save Biscuit. Dr. Dodds is one of my veterinarian heroes along with Dr. Fowler, avian experts

Dr. Greg and Linda Harrison, and oncologist Dr. Greg Ogilvie.

I'd known Dr. Dodds for over thirty years, and despite her schedule, she always responded to my calls. I outlined Brix's case, and I could practically hear her excitement through the phone.

"Oh Doug, this is going to be such a fun challenge," she said. "I bet the problem is in the signaling from her hypothalamus to the adrenal glands. Her sodium and potassium are normal, so part of the adrenals work. I'd try prednisone to mimic cortisol release, and support her adrenals with supplements. And of course, feed whole foods."

The hypothalamus, nestled near the pituitary, is a command center for feel-good chemicals, like those that bring a surfer's "stoke." If the entire hypothalamus had been destroyed, Brix wouldn't be alive. But if just the appetite center had been damaged, and we could mimic its messaging chemically, we had a shot.

We started her on prednisone to stimulate hunger and added a glandular supplement called Standard Process Canine Adrenal Support. Brix, still disinterested in food, received hand-fed Biscuit Balls loaded with nutrients and medication.

Nothing happened for a week.

Then, one morning, Debbie, our vibrant tech from Trinidad, was hand-feeding Biscuit when Biscuit spat out her meatball with some force. As Debbie reached for it, she noticed Brix had wandered out of her kennel and was eating it. Debbie shrieked loud enough to be heard across the hospital: "Brix just ate a Biscuit Ball!" She picked Brix up and kissed her, tears in her eyes.

We weren't sure if it was a fluke or a turning point. But the next day, Brix ate two more meatballs. Then six. Then, a week later, she ate her first full meal from a bowl. If I'd had champagne, I would've toasted the whole team right there.

We still didn't know her long-term prognosis. Prednisone has significant side effects, especially immune suppression, muscle wasting, and liver damage. We'd need to counter those with a meticulous diet, supplements, and immune support. But the fact that she was eating was everything.

Caroline and David returned with one of their three athletic grown sons to bring Brix home. David, it turned out, was also a UC Davis alum with a degree in agricultural economics. Both he and Caroline hailed from Idaho before falling in love with San Clemente. David loved fly fishing, and one of their sons surfed Mavericks, one of the scariest big waves in the world.

I couldn't offer them a timeline. A week? A year? Maybe ten if everything went perfectly. The protocol would require heroic dedication.

Years passed.

Just a few weeks ago, Caroline returned to the clinic with Tug, their massive, goofy, champion Portuguese water dog, brought in as Brix's companion. Tug, blessed with good genetics, became a show-ring sensation, winning ribbons and medals. But after a brief show career, the Westendorfs retired him so he could just be a dog.

As I examined Tug, who licked my face enthusiastically, I saw her.

Brix.

Nestled behind him, healthy and alert. She had just turned fourteen.

Fourteen.

Against every expert's prediction, Brix had thrived because she landed in the right hands with the right family and the right kind of veterinary magic. Dr. Dodds's guidance, a holistic protocol, and the Westendorfs' bottomless well of love and effort gave Brix the life she was meant to live.

Without all of that, Brix would have been just a memory at four months old.

CHAPTER 25

TORTOISES AND TOXINS

I enjoy working with tortoises. I've treated many that were presumed dead and came back to life, unlike birds and rabbits, which often die suddenly and rarely can be revived. I vividly remember my vet school classmate's tortoise coming back from the grave after Dr. Fowler declared him dead following a long surgery and placed him in the cooler during my fourth-year rotation in the zoological ward. When my classmate came to check on her tortoise's recovery, she pulled him from the cooler and began CPR, praying and pleading. Dr. Fowler, the expert who had written the textbooks on zoological medicine, had already tried CPR before pronouncing him deceased. Two hours later, the tortoise started moving and walked around the treatment room as if nothing had happened. Because of that memory, I never declared a desert tortoise dead until twenty-four hours had passed.

One busy Saturday afternoon, a family returned home from soccer games to find their beloved forty-five-year-old California desert tortoise, Panzer, lifeless at the bottom of their pool. As always, we tried to revive him with CPR, medications, and acupuncture stimulation under the nostrils. We gave Lasix to draw fluid from his lungs, inserted a breathing tube, and manually ventilated him for hours with no signs of life. I left the clinic late that night, leaving a note for the Sunday technician that Panzer was "presumed dead."

The next morning, our pre-vet tech Greg called. "Hi Dr. Coward," he said. "I wanted to know what I should do for the 'presumed dead' Panzer. He didn't read the note. He's alive, walking. And hungry!"

Panzer is still alive today, a testament to the remarkable resilience of tortoises.

Tortoise surgeries are both thrilling and challenging due to their shells. At Doc's practice, we averaged one such procedure a week. Abdominal surgeries to remove bladder stones, intestinal obstructions, or assist egg-bound females were the most intense. I remember one trifecta surgery: we removed a large nail from a tortoise's intestines, a three-inch bladder stone, and a dozen retained eggs. The thirty-five-year-old female had presented only for anorexia.

We used a Dremel to cut a rectangle from her plastron, the shell covering her belly, which we soaked in saline to keep the living tissue viable. From there, the surgery resembled any mammal's exploratory. We cut along the *linea alba*, God's gift to surgeons for being a poorly vascularized tissue seam that allows a clean incision with little bleeding. We removed the nail, bladder stone, and reproductive organs, then sutured the muscles and secured the shell with fiberglass. The tortoise was placed in a sling to keep her from sticking to her bedding while the shell healed.

Anesthesia in tortoises is tricky. The difference between too light, just right, and overdosed is razor thin. Too light, and their limbs flail in pain; too deep, and they may never wake. Thankfully, we had skilled anesthesia techs like Sherrie, Rosa, and Juan, whose instincts were vital.

Forty-five is not old for a tortoise. One of our patients—a 106-year-old California desert tortoise—still comes in annually. Tortoises, like many parrots, age without physical decline, a phenomenon called negligible senescence. One Aldabra tortoise recently celebrated what is believed to be his 190th birthday, still vibrant. Scientists are eager to understand their longevity and apply it to human health.

After Panzer's miraculous recovery, his family brought us a baby tortoise named Sweetie as a gift. She was charming from the start, happily munching salad greens, hibiscus, and chopped vegetables. When the sun was out, we put her outside, carefully watching for overheating. As she grew, she spent more time outdoors.

By age seven, Sweetie had developed a routine. Visitors were astonished to hear her tapping at the sliding glass door, wanting in. Once inside, she'd trot to the fridge, expectantly waiting for salad. Normally, she fed herself from our garden. Strawberries, kale, carrot tops, lettuce, and her favorite, hibiscus flowers.

One Sunday morning, I found her in the garden, unresponsive, eyes closed. An odd smell lingered in the air. I rushed her to the clinic. My hands shake when it's my own pet, so Greg took over. We went through our emergency ABCDEF protocol: airway, breathing, circulation, drugs, exhale (pause and assess), and fluids.

Greg passed a stomach tube, carefully avoiding the windpipe, and delivered 6 cc of vegetable juice, 1 cc of echinacea, and an herbal detox blend of milk thistle, dandelion, and burdock. We gave subcutaneous fluids with B vitamins and vitamin C. We noticed a slight eyelid twitch following dexamethasone for shock. After twenty minutes, she began breathing on her own. I quietly thanked God.

Two hours later, she began to move. We collected blood, and her liver values were catastrophically high, classic signs of acute poisoning. I remembered the strange smell from the garden. Sweetie was transferred to our exotic ward, a temperature-controlled haven Nancy had built with cages fit for everything from macaws to turtles. We warmed her to help her cold-blooded metabolism detoxify. She would need weeks of care: tube feedings, herbs, fluids. The liver, thankfully, is forgiving. Even two-thirds of it can regenerate in three weeks. That's about how long it took Sweetie.

After she stabilized, I spoke with our next-door neighbors. Their gardener had sprayed their yard with Roundup the Friday before, assuring them it was "safe for pets." That story is tragically common. Winds had carried the spray into the garden. Sweetie had ingested a nearly lethal dose. She didn't wash her vegetables as we did.

Avoiding toxins and eating detoxifying plant foods or herbs are two of the most important steps both ends of the leash can take to protect the liver. As I learned at holistic conferences, the keys to health for all species are a thriving microbiome and a well-functioning liver. Real food heals both. Highly processed, industrial food harms both and contributes to the chronic diseases we see in pets and people alike.

CHAPTER 26

FOOD THERAPY FOR MAX & BRADY

Thanks to the dozens of books on human alternative cancer care I had studied, we developed an integrative anticancer protocol for pets. Many of these books were written by physicians who, after receiving terminal diagnoses, turned to alternative therapies out of desperation, and survived. Their experiences gave me hope that food and supplements could offer a gentle yet powerful approach to treating cancer in animals, especially as more patients were being diagnosed and families increasingly asked for integrative options.

The first patient I tried this protocol on was a spirited Jack Russell terrier named Max, owned by the equally spirited and devoted couple, Sherrie and Brad Parker. Max had presented with a bleeding tumor outside and inside his rectum. We discussed the full range of options: surgery, food therapy, and a referral to Dr. Ogilvie, the renowned integrative oncologist in Carlsbad. While unsure about invasive treatments, the Parkers were immediately open to food therapy. It was noninvasive, safe, and free from the painful side effects so often seen with radiation, surgery, and chemotherapy.

Max was already active, but I encouraged them to take him running on the beach to enhance the healing process through "earthing"—the grounding, antioxidant benefits of direct contact with the earth, especially by the ocean. The fresh sea air, rich in oxygen, is a natural enemy to cancer, and running barefoot or paw-bare connects living beings to the restorative energy of the earth.

A few weeks later, the Parkers returned for a recheck.

"It took us a while to decide," Brad said, "but we're ready to go ahead with surgery."

I was always cautious with surgeries involving the rear end. It's a sensitive area and prone to infection. But when I examined Max, I was stunned. The large, ulcerated, walnut-sized tumor that had been both internal and external just three weeks before had shrunk dramatically. What remained was a small, raisin-sized mass on the outer margin of the rectum. Internally, the tumor was gone.

I gloved up and palpated inside. Nothing. The remaining mass was easy to remove, and Max recovered fully, without complications or infection.

That moment marked a turning point: We began to trust that food and supplements, when thoughtfully chosen and used alongside or even in place of conventional therapies, could indeed change the trajectory of a cancer diagnosis.

Since then, countless families have asked if the anticancer protocol we use for pets could work for humans too. I always direct them to *Anticancer: A New Way of Life*, a remarkable book that bridges medical science and holistic wisdom, offering hope and a path forward for anyone facing the challenge of cancer.

Shortly after Max's success, another memorable case entered our clinic: a four-year-old border collie named Brady. He was the beloved companion of Josh and Lindsey, a newlywed couple who looked like they'd stepped out of a romance novel. Sadly, their perfect life was disrupted by Brady's chronic, bloody diarrhea, an affliction that had plagued him for over a year. Despite visits to multiple board-certified specialists and numerous treatments, Brady's condition continued to worsen. He was being kept alive by weekly blood transfusions.

His medical file was thick and full of dead ends. Every possible cause had been investigated: parasites, toxic ingestion, food allergies, stress colitis, even intestinal lymphoma. Exploratory surgeries and biopsies had all come back inconclusive, most noting probable lymphoma, unresponsive to treatment. The last recommendation was euthanasia.

During our first exam, I asked about his diet. Brady was on a prescription food of hydrolyzed soy protein, corn starch, hydrolyzed chicken liver, and unspecified vegetable oil. None of it was whole food, and it likely contained GMOs and pro-inflammatory ingredients. No one had yet recommended a fresh food diet. When I suggested turkey with carrots, broccoli, and sweet potatoes, the couple eagerly agreed.

We added grass-fed bovine colostrum, Nutrigest with soothing ginger, high-quality fish oil, and kept Brady on his corticosteroids and Flagyl. I told them I wasn't sure this would work, but I'd reach out to integrative experts for guidance.

Dr. Jean Dodds, author of *Canine Nutrigenomics*, quickly responded. She affirmed our food and supplement choices and recommended giving it three weeks. I also contacted the Chi Institute of Chinese Veterinary Medicine, where a consultant recommended a centuries-old herbal remedy called The Great Saussurea, specifically for hemorrhagic colitis, which had a cooling and anti-inflammatory effect on the intestines. She exclaimed enthusiastically that "the basis of traditional Chinese veterinary medicine is first and foremost food therapy."

Brady devoured the food. Within days, Lindsey noticed less blood in his stool. Within weeks, he improved dramatically. His coat grew soft and shiny, he gained weight, and he never needed another transfusion. What began as a longshot turned into a breakthrough. This case deepened my conviction that food—real, healing, intentional food—can be powerful medicine.

I couldn't wait to begin formal training in food therapy. There was so much more to learn, and so many more patients who needed hope. I enrolled in the Chi Institute to further equip my toolbelt with integrated wellness techniques.

CHAPTER 27

TCVM

O ne of the finest animal trainers I know came into the practice with an unusual request. Lynn Sheedy had trained golden retriever companions and guide dogs for severely disabled college students. These remarkable dogs became beloved figures on campus, escorting students in wheelchairs to class, opening and closing classroom doors, even paying for lunch with dollar bills and collecting change.

Tall, athletic, and always joyful, Lynn was my age and debating between settling full time in Baja California or returning to the Saddleback Valley. When she arrived that day without any dogs, she asked if I had a few minutes. Her eyes sparkled with excitement. "Dr. Doug, I'm training to become an animal communicator. Would you mind if I practiced on your dog and a few patients?"

Curious, I asked how one becomes an animal communicator. I had known a few, including Terri Steuben and Renata Halvusrude, who said they were born with a telepathic ability to hear animals. But Lynn had taken a different path. "I've been studying for a while," she explained. "I got so drained training dogs that I had to find another way to serve. My instructor says anyone can learn this. You just have to clear your mind completely, focus, and one day you start hearing them."

I joked that clearing my mind was nearly impossible as my thoughts ran wild even while meditating. But I gave Lynn the go-ahead. The staff, who respected Lynn deeply, were happy to help. I left out that she was now training to be a communicator.

Before she entered the treatment room, Lynn asked if I had any questions for Rudy, our beloved family dog. "Actually, yes," I said. "Can you ask him why he eats his poop?"

Rudy was a notorious poop snacker. While it saved us some yard cleanup, his habit of licking visitors' faces afterward was less appreciated. I cringed every time someone bent down to let Rudy greet them.

I forgot all about Lynn until the end of the day. She returned with a report. "Thanks, Dr. Doug. The blind boa told me he prefers gray mice to white ones. Most dogs and cats just wanted to know why they were here and when they'd be going home. But Rudy—he was special. He told me he loves the clinic. He says he's like Dr. Phil because he reassures all the patients, tells them when they'll be fed and walked, and reminds them that everyone here is helping them. Sometimes, though, he says he gets exhausted and has to 'go out of body' for a while."

I raised an eyebrow at that one.

She continued, "He says he feels healthy except for itchy eyes, and the eye medicine makes them itch more. He likes his food and says his main job now is taking care of Shawn since Kelly went to college. And he wants you to stop working so late. He says he smacks your leg to tell you it's time to go home, but when you ignore him, he barks at Luke until you put him away. If you still won't listen, he poops and pees nearby to get your attention."

It was uncanny. Everything she said was true. Rudy had always pawed at me when the clinic was quiet and I was working through lab results. He never barked or acted this way at home.

"And about the poop-eating?" I asked.

"He said, 'Why not?'" Lynn replied with a shrug.

I wasn't impressed until she added, "He also said he wants liver in his food."

My aversion to liver came from childhood trauma. My mom used to fry it and force me to eat it. I would never feed this putrid organ of detoxification to Rudy. But later, after hearing the many benefits of liver during the study of traditional Chinese veterinary medicine food therapy, especially for dogs with the many maladies Rudy suffered from, I changed my tune. Rudy ate liver for the rest of his life.

That same week, I attended a food therapy course at the Chi Institute, which is known for TCVM: traditional Chinese veterinary medicine. The food therapy chart, initially a blur of foreign concepts, became my trusted guide. Every being eats, and food has the power to heal. Drugs treat symptoms, whereas food restores balance and cures.

I put my new knowledge to the test as soon as I returned to work. A surfer friend referred his neighbor, Sue, whose Rottweiler, Odin, had chronic diarrhea. Her vet recommended a biopsy, which terrified her. She feared anesthesia would harm or kill him.

When I entered the exam room, Odin lunged at me. Sue, calm and strong, restrained him. "He's just miserable," she said. "I know he's hurting. I just don't want to make it worse."

I understood completely. I explained the TCVM approach: treating syndromes, not just diseases. Odin's symptoms pointed to internal heat: inflamed ears, red tongue, rapid heartbeat, raw rectum. His dry kibble, with chicken as the main ingredient, only added to the inflammation.

Using the new TCVM food therapy chart I now had memorized, I designed a cooling, anti-inflammatory diet of turkey, white fish, spinach, broccoli, sweet potatoes, and berries. I eliminated inflammatory foods like chicken and white rice and added Nutrigest and colostrum to soothe and repair the gut.

Sue left with notes, a chart, and a grocery list. Miraculously, Odin improved. His coat became shiny, his weight increased, and his stools normalized. We later added Missing Link and fish oils for additional anti-inflammatory support. Odin reached a healthy ninety pounds and was once again a happy, strong dog.

This experience affirmed everything I had just learned. TCVM was more than theory. It was transformative in practice. From Rudy's poetic wisdom to Odin's healing journey, I saw firsthand how food is more than fuel. It's *medicine.*

CHAPTER 28

PICKLE'S PICKLE

The best animal model for our health crisis of "diabe-sity" and COVID isn't a rat, rabbit, or dog, but the finicky feline. Cats thrive and heal on real food as nature intended, not food cooked for thirty minutes in a factory at two hundred degrees. People differ slightly from felines in that we benefit from gentle cooking, which allows opti-mal digestion and absorption of nutrients. Our genes and bodies were designed for a hunter-gatherer/herds-man life, just as cats are designed to hunt, kill, and digest fresh rodents. Nothing in our exquisite design, nor that of felines, has changed in tens of thousands of years from our Paleolithic anatomy and physiology.

Today, both pets and people have deviated from their ancestral diets and lifestyles, leading to an epidemic of illness. We Americans eat addictive, factory-made food that leaves us too sick, too painful, and too tired to move. Cats don't cook their rodents in the wild. Factory-created cat food, cooked at high temperatures and loaded with cheap meat, carbohydrates, and preservatives, causes the same damage to felines that junk food does to people. Feed a species an unnatural diet and you will get unnatu-ral disease.

Dr. Robert Lustig, a brilliant pediatric endocrinologist at UCSF with forty years of experience, has bravely asserted that the cause of chronic, noninfectious diseases in people is highly processed food. The cure, he says, is simple: eat real food. Endocrinologists are the intellectuals of the medical world. They study the effects of hormones released from one part of the body and how they act on another. They are medical ecologists who understand the body as a whole. Dr. Lustig was shocked to see adult diseases, like type 2 diabetes and fatty liver, emerging in obese children. These illnesses, he said, are "foodable, not drugable." His treatment wasn't more insulin or liver transplants. It was feeding real food. His book *Metabolical* should be required reading for all medical and veterinary students. I guarantee that within four weeks of switching to a real food diet, an obese pet or person will feel like moving off the couch and getting outdoors.

In 1979, I observed lions, cheetahs, and leopards in Kenya from the jeep of an Aussie wildlife photographer who picked us up while hitchhiking. These big cats were lean, muscular, and thriving on raw prey. By contrast, as a clueless vet student in 1981, I was taught that industrial pet food was optimal for health, even though wild animals I'd seen were never fed anything but whole food.

The patients I saw at Doc's dermatology practice looked terrible compared to wild dogs and wild cats in Africa and India. My food epiphany came from a gorgeous Labrador in the wine country and the miraculous results of a whole food diet on my dog, cat, bird, and rat patients.

I was surprised I'd never shared this knowledge with Nancy's sister, Marcy, and her animal-loving family. They were surrounded by wildlife near Monterey Bay and had birds, cats, and dogs. My niece Kaylan called me in February 2020, just before I was headed overseas for a conference, asking if I could look at her cat, Pickles, who was limping and not improving despite antibiotics and anti-inflammatories. I stopped by her home in San Diego and was shocked to see how obese Pickles was. He was being fed an expensive chicken-based kibble.

At UC Davis we were taught, "common diseases occur commonly." In obese cats, limping is usually from a fall or bite wound. But I couldn't find evidence of a bite. I suspected an injury exacerbated by excess weight and inflammatory food. He also had a growth on his nose. I recommended switching to a real food diet of 80 percent ground turkey and 20 percent cooked colorful vegetables. I explained the anti-inflammatory and healing properties of plant pigments and the slow weaning process from kibble.

I was confident the diet would reduce his weight and inflammation. I was wrong.

What emerged over the next week was dire. Nancy and Marcy visited Kaylan and saw that Pickles was now limping on all four legs, wheezing, and had a dramatically enlarged nose lump. He was drinking and urinating excessively. They drove him ninety minutes to our clinic in Mission Viejo. Blood tests, x-rays, and a biopsy revealed fuzzy joints, cloudy lungs, and a nasal mass, all symptoms indicative of either systemic infection, cancer, or autoimmune disease. The lab identified the nasal growth as Histoplasma, a rare fungus never before seen in California cats. Blood tests also showed diabetes and kidney disease.

Pickles, a strictly indoor cat, had somehow developed a fungus only found in moist, bat-and-bird-dropping-laced soil along the Mississippi River Valley. With his immune system compromised by kibble, he was vulnerable.

Dr. Birgit Ankone, our feline integrative specialist, initiated IV antifungal Amphotericin B, the only treatment that might save Pickles's life. The treatment was aggressive but stressful. Pickles, once gentle, became frantic during clinic visits after his long drive from San Diego. I ended the hospital-based treatments and transitioned him to Kaylan's loving home care with oral antifungals, colostrum, and glandular immune support supplements.

Slowly, Pickles recovered. The diabetes reversed. The limp and nasal bump vanished. His breathing normalized. His weight dropped. Pickles became the goofy, affectionate feline he once was.

Had Pickles died, his cause of death would have been listed as Histoplasmosis. But the real culprit was his kibble-based diet, or the feline version of the human SAD diet (basically high-carb junk food). His immune and endocrine systems were hijacked. A single spore, which a healthy cat would have overcome, nearly killed him.

Every diabetic cat I've treated was a kibble eater. Every one of them recovered on whole food.

People and pets alike are not designed to graze on junk food all day. This constant snacking overwhelms insulin receptors and bypasses natural satiety cues like leptin, creating a cycle of hunger, obesity, and disease. Fat cells become inflammatory factories. Obesity makes breathing difficult and immune function impaired, whether in a feline with fungus or a person with COVID.

Pickles didn't die because we treated both the symptom and the cause. His diet changed. His environment changed. He was loved into healing. If even one person reading this changes their diet, and their pet's diet, to whole food, then Pickles's suffering served a purpose.

CHAPTER 29

WHAT'S LOVE GOT TO DO WITH IT

I arrived at work after Dawn Patrol surfing followed by thirty minutes of meditation. It had already been a great day. When I glanced at the appointment book, I noticed that some close friends from San Clemente were coming in with Zoe, their fourteen-year-old wire-haired fox terrier. Zoe's original elderly owner had passed away in 2002, and her adult children, overwhelmed by demanding careers, surrendered her to their local veterinary hospital's adoption program. That's where Chris Thornburg and Kristi Dassonville entered her life.

California transplants from Bozeman, Montana, Chris and Kristi adored wire-haired fox terriers and had been hoping to adopt one. When they read about Zoe in a local Saddleback Valley paper, they knew she was the one. Their adoption meeting confirmed the connection. Zoe immediately bonded with the couple, and they with her. Since then, they had cared for Zoe with wholehearted devotion, following our wellness guidelines by feeding her a whole food diet fortified with Missing Link and fish oils. Zoe stayed lean, muscular, and joyful, which was a pleasure to see socially or on the walking trails of San Clemente. Until today.

When they arrived, Kristi was visibly distressed and sobbing, something I'd never seen before. She was usually upbeat, with a radiant smile and a laugh that could fill a room. Raised near the rivers of Bozeman, she was a skilled trout fisher and an accomplished architect. Her joy was usually contagious. Today, she was heartbroken. Chris, always fashion-forward and coolly composed, looked shaken. Though he worked as a Hollywood graphic artist for Warner Brothers and traveled the world designing fashion, there was nothing superficial about him. He was kind, grounded, and deeply loving.

"There was nothing unusual yesterday," Kristi said through tears. "But this morning, Zoe vomited, stumbled, and started acting drunk. Now she's too weak to walk. We haven't changed anything in her environment. How did this happen?"

"We'll take a look and run some blood tests," I said gently. "There are many possibilities—liver or kidney issues are high on the list, especially at her age. When those organs fail to filter toxins, the body behaves like it's been poisoned."

Zoe's gums were pale, but not gravely so. Her eyes were clear. Her heart sounded normal. I palpated her abdomen. The intestines, kidneys, liver, and bladder felt unremarkable. She wasn't in visible pain. But when I gently lifted the skin over her neck, it stayed tented, which is an indicator of dehydration.

We brought Zoe to the treatment area to start intravenous fluids, take x-rays, and run blood tests. I knew separation from her family would stress her, so we placed Chris in a quiet room with Zoe and connected her to a fluid pump. Our techs, Juan and Rosa, had the test results within the hour: stage 4 kidney failure.

Kristi had returned to work, so I broke the news to Chris. "Does she have any chance of recovery?" he asked quietly.

"We'll know more in a few days," I said. "If we can flush out the toxins and get her eating again, there's hope."

Chris nodded. "They told us when we adopted her that Zoe was the smartest dog they'd ever seen. Let's hope she's just as strong."

That day, we administered IV fluids and later gave 600 mL subcutaneously so Zoe could sleep at home. Chris brought her back first thing the next morning. She hadn't vomited but was still too weak to eat. Throughout the day, Chris remained at her side, gently stroking her fur. Raquel, one of our most joyful and compassionate pre-vet students, oversaw Zoe's care.

Raquel, always laughing and full of warmth, asked Chris if she could try some soft food with Zoe. As she and Chris comforted her, Zoe lifted her head and took a bite. Then another. Chris's face lit up. Raquel was ecstatic. It was a small miracle and the first sign of recovery.

Still, I remembered lectures from a Waikiki conference about kidney disease. Zoe's stage of disease was at the five minutes before midnight on the kidney clock. We gave her additional fluids before she went home again. Chris and Kristi faced a choice: euthanasia or learning to administer fluids at home. They chose the latter.

We taught them how to place the needle, open the fluid line, calculate volume, and ensure comfort. It's a challenging, emotional task for pet parents, but they took it on with grace. Soon, they were giving daily treatments, knowing that even missing one day caused Zoe to decline.

A few weeks later, I saw Chris walking Zoe. She was alert, tail wagging, full of life. I was stunned, and cautious. I expected her kidneys to fail again by September. But Zoe defied the odds.

She thrived that summer in Montana and through the fall and winter in San Clemente. By spring, she was receiving 800 mL of fluids daily and was still spirited and eating well. Only once before had I seen this kind of reversal in Juno, a geriatric husky with metastatic lung cancer who survived a year on a whole food anticancer diet, immune supplements, and sheer willpower. I expected Juno to live a week at most. Like Juno, Zoe had hit the wall and rebounded.

Eventually, Zoe began to slow down. By August 2016, she could no longer walk unaided and had trouble sleeping. Chris and Kristi, ever devoted, recognized the signs of suffering: distant stares, labored painful movements, and frequent accidents.

They didn't let her suffer. On August 21, a Bozeman vet helped ease her passing.

I often reflect on Zoe and Juno's stories. Their longevity wasn't just medicine. It was love, fresh food, daily movement, laughter, nature, and spirit. Most of all, it was the unwavering commitment of families who believed in healing beyond the conventional. I used to think I'd never know why these patients defied the odds. I was wrong.

The answer is everything we already know: it's nature, nourishment, and love.

CHAPTER 30

RABBIT'S RADICAL RESPONSE

If I wanted more evidence for how to defy the odds, I didn't have to look further than the window of Warwick's bookstore in La Jolla. The store always displays a few of their favorite new books and announces when authors will be in town for readings and signings. This moment happened just after I returned from the 2019 Surfers Medical Association annual conference. At that meeting, two different MDs referenced studies on rabbits and heart disease. One spoke about the impact of a high-carb junk food (SAD) diet on rabbit hearts and its parallel to the obesity epidemic in children caused by high fructose corn syrup. The other discussed how statins affected rabbits with high cholesterol. I kept thinking how odd it was to use rabbits, animals that, in my experience, rarely get heart disease. In contrast, dogs and cats suffer from various heart conditions but never coronary artery disease, which is so common in humans.

When I learned all the rabbits had been euthanized for researchers to study their hearts, it made economic sense. They're inexpensive and easy to handle. But having cared for rescued rabbits over the years, the thought saddened me. If the goal was to understand heart disease in people, why not use dye studies in junk-food-eating human volunteers instead of sacrificing bunnies?

The book that caught my attention in the window was *The Rabbit Effect*. On its yellow cover was an EKG line shaped like rabbit ears and the subtitle *Live Longer, Happier, and Healthier with the Groundbreaking Science of Kindness*. The author was Kelli Harding, MD, MPH. I was intrigued. I walked inside, found it in the science section, and was captivated by the frequent mention of animal studies. I bought the book and read it that week.

Dr. Harding experienced a paradigm shift after reading about a 1986 New Zealand rabbit study, and so did I. The study was well-controlled and used male New Zealand white rabbits known to develop heart disease when fed a high-fat diet. Researchers aimed to prove a link between cholesterol and heart disease. All rabbits were fed the same diet, and after several months, researchers measured their cholesterol, heart rate, and blood pressure. As expected, all cholesterol levels were high. But under the microscope, one group had 60 percent fewer fatty deposits in their arteries, without a clear scientific reason.

Eventually, the researchers discovered that all the healthier rabbits had been cared for by a single Canadian PhD known for her gentle, affectionate approach. She cuddled, spoke to, and spent extra time with the animals in her care. It was a shocking revelation: loving care seemed to change biology. The lead researcher repeated the experiment under controlled conditions, assigning rabbits either to the kind caregiver or to a more mechanical, impersonal one. Once again, the rabbits who received affection had significantly healthier arteries. The study was published in *Science*.

I had read *The Secret Life of Plants* in 1974 and knew plants respond to kindness. But this rabbit study made me reflect on animals in distress—and two patients came to mind: Luna with her cancer-ridden lungs and Zoe with her failing kidneys. I had seen them defy odds and live well beyond their prognoses. Could kindness be the reason?

I called Chris to ask about Zoe's home care. Everything he described matched the so-called Rabbit Effect. The couple was united, gentle, and tender in their care. Often, families are torn apart when deciding whether to euthanize a terminally ill pet. Renowned animal communicator Terri Steuben has said animals can sense conflicting thoughts and become confused when one family member wants them to stay and another is ready to let go.

In 2004, I witnessed something extraordinary during a routine quality-of-life discussion. A longtime client couple brought in their thirteen-year-old golden retriever, Kirby. She wagged her tail, but her breathing was labored. After an exam, I suggested x-rays and blood tests to rule out pneumonia, heart disease, or possibly cancer. The husband, a busy attorney, agreed. But his wife abruptly interrupted, saying, "I've made up my mind. I won't allow Kirby to go through any tests. It's her time to go to Heaven. She's been the best dog I've ever had, and I don't want her to suffer anymore. We're going to put her to sleep."

There was silence. Then Kirby looked at her husband, then me, and finally locked eyes with the wife, for ten long seconds. Then she died. On the exam table. I was stunned. I had never seen a dog pass at that moment, as if responding to her person's declaration. I checked her heart. She was gone.

Zoe, on the other hand, lived on because Chris and Kristi were completely aligned in their decision to care for her. They prepared everything: a towel, measured fluids, turkey slices in the fridge. Kristi would hold and comfort Zoe while Chris inserted the needle and monitored the drip. Some days, they stopped short of the full 800 mL because they sensed Zoe had had enough. Other days, she received the full dose. Zoe always remained calm, and afterward, she'd jump up and run to the fridge, tail wagging.

Their home was a sanctuary of kindness and ritual. I became convinced that their loving touch and intentional care altered Zoe's physiology. Instead of succumbing to kidney failure, she thrived for eighteen more months.

This, I now believe, is the true Rabbit Effect: kindness that alters biology. I had always taught that healthy food, exercise, sleep, meditation, hydration, and clean air were pillars of health.

But I now believe that loving kindness may trump them all.

PART FOUR:
HEALING BOTH ENDS
OF THE LEASH

CHAPTER 31

TOXICITY AT BOTH ENDS OF THE LEASH

As a result of my love for the outdoors and veterinary medicine, I've been foolishly exposed to a heavy toxic load. It's no wonder my hearing is compromised and I battle autoimmune diseases.

At age fifteen, I wanted to backpack into the High Sierras with my high school buddies who had already made several week-long adventures. To do that, I needed a down sleeping bag, hiking boots, a stove, and a backpack. That meant I needed a better-paying job than refereeing peewee basketball games.

Around that time, my brother Dave offered me a job at a local live Christmas tree farm. A Little League teammate's dad, a UC Berkeley forestry professor, had started a living tree farm in the hills of Moraga and needed labor to plant thousands of Monterey pines. Dave recruited his friends, and reluctantly, me. Known as the "play-a-holic" in the family, I was a last resort.

We were handed shovels and began digging holes for seedlings. As the youngest, I was given the backbreaking job of planting the trees and moving from row to row. We were also tasked with spraying paraquat, a lethal herbicide, on weed patches. Dave's buddies would sometimes spray me as a prank; I'd retaliate and get caught, wasting precious chemicals. I did this for two years until I was fired for "double planting" seedlings under pressure from the older boys, who threatened me if I didn't comply. The boss noticed and let me go. We had no idea how close we came to serious harm. Just a spoonful of paraquat can kill a human. Even low-level exposure damages lungs and has been linked to Parkinson's disease in farm workers. We wore no gloves or masks and never washed before lunch.

Despite the dangers, I made enough to outfit myself for years of backpacking adventures.

My next toxic venture was a summer job at a fluorescent paint factory, taken to buy scuba gear. The factory reeked of chemicals. Workers wore gas masks while pouring fresh paint into drying trays. Once dried, the pigment was ground and processed into fluorescent sheets. Dust coated everything. I was covered in bright red, orange, and yellow powders. The chemicals leaked into nearby San Francisco Bay, killing fish and alerting the EPA.

My body fought back. I worked out intensely for basketball season and coughed up pigment during summer league games. My skin oozed it. Later, I'd learn in dermatology class that the skin acts as a "third kidney," aiding detoxification. Thankfully, daily full-court basketball opened pores and flushed toxins through sweat. I credit that regimen with my survival.

Had I known then what I know now, I would have flushed myself with water. "The solution to pollution is dilution," Dr. Fowler often said in toxicology class. Sadly, we weren't encouraged to drink water during games or practice in high school or at Santa Clara. After practice, our only option was soda, which was a forbidden fruit in our household due to my dad's best friend, a dentist, warning against it. The thought of cavities sent me running from the cola dispenser.

My patients are also bombarded by toxins, starting with factory-made food. Large pet food companies must only meet the Association of American Feed Control Officials' (AAFCO) minimum nutritional standards, guidelines developed for slaughter animals, not longevity. Pets are classified the same as livestock. AAFCO's definition of "adequate" is equivalent to a passing grade. Enough to survive, not thrive.

For true vitality, food must protect the liver and feed the microbiome—the trillions of beneficial microbes working in our intestines. Highly processed food harms both. Kibble only has to meet basic protein, carbohydrate, and fat ratios similar to the contents of a piece of leather. During vet school summers I played basketball and worked in a parasitology lab in Townsville, Australia. I went weekly to a slaughterhouse, collecting a parasitic worm causing river blindness in humans. We harvested the parasites from nodules in condemned meat, or meat labeled for pet food. Roadkill and even euthanized animals were rumored to be part of the mix. That meat became kibble.

The kibble-making process involves high heat and prolonged cooking, triggering the Maillard reaction—responsible for the browned flavor in crusty bread, seared steak, and toasted marshmallows. This reaction creates Advanced Glycation End Products, or AGEs, which inflame intestines, joints, skin, and the brain. AGEs contribute to the chronic diseases I see in pets: diarrhea, arthritis, itchy skin, seizures, and cancer.

Thankfully, whole foods can reverse this damage. Excellent nutrition and lifestyle choices have been shown to override genetic predispositions. Epigenetics, the study of how environment and lifestyle influence gene expression, shows that genes account for just 10 percent of our fate. Lifestyle accounts for the other 90 percent. What we feed ourselves and our pets is the single most powerful choice we make. We can either nurture the microbiome and liver with real food, or poison them with AGEs and chemical additives like Roundup.

In 2015, my veterinary hero Dr. Jean Dodds published *Canine Nutrigenomics: The New Science of Feeding Your Dog for Optimum Health*. She details how the right food and supplements, paired with healthy choices, can even reverse genetic issues like hip dysplasia. Nutrients surrounding DNA can influence what genes express or suppress. Conversely, poor food can mutate healthy genes. I often wonder if I'd have been six feet, five inches tall and injury-free in college had I eaten and slept optimally during my teens.

More on epigenetics to come, and particularly the transformative power of integrated wellness on gene expression in both pets and people.

CHAPTER 32

CANCER AT BOTH ENDS OF THE LEASH

I was shocked by the amount of cancer I encountered during my first experience in pet practice. As a zoology and wildlife veterinary student, I had primarily worked with wild and zoo animals who ate real food. In that environment, I had only seen one cancer case—a young African gray parrot with a genetic form of bone cancer. But in pet practice, cancer was rampant across many species.

I had no interest or skill in treating cancer with chemotherapy or radiation. I left those treatments to experts like Dr. Greg Ogilvie in nearby Carlsbad and my cousin Randy, an oncologist at the Mayo Clinic. I often called Randy for advice when family or friends were diagnosed with cancer.

In vet school, we were never taught that food could help prevent or treat cancer, or even relieve arthritis. Yet, I had witnessed hundreds of dogs with severe arthritis return to normal function on a whole food diet and a few supplements. Still, it never occurred to me that food could play a role in cancer recovery.

To my surprise, systems of healing such as Ayurvedic medicine in India, traditional Chinese medicine, and macrobiotic practices in Japan had been using real food to treat and even cure cancer for centuries. I called Randy in the 1980s to ask what he knew about food as a cancer therapy. Based on his training and experience at the Mayo Clinic, he told me there was no scientific foundation for such an approach.

How times have changed. Today, the Mayo Clinic website includes integrative care for cancer patients. In 2017, they even published a book on the topic. Alongside conventional tools like chemotherapy and radiation, they now offer dietary therapy, meditation, biofeedback, exercise counseling, and spiritual reconnection. There's even a detailed list of cancer-fighting foods and an article titled "How Plant-Based Foods Help Fight Cancer." Conversely, grilled and processed meats have been shown to significantly increase cancer risk.

I've read hundreds of books on cancer, because one in four dogs and one in five cats will develop it. Almost half of all dogs over ten will die from cancer. I remember attending a Padres baseball game in 2005 and being stunned when dozens of childhood cancer survivors were introduced before the game. I had never even heard of a child getting cancer when I was growing up—now it seemed as common as chicken pox. Clearly, something in our modern environment has gone very wrong. I place much of the blame on the rise of highly processed food over the past fifty years.

One of the most powerful books I've read, and the one I most often recommend to clients, is *Anticancer: A New Way of Life* by Dr. David Servan-Schreiber. Part memoir, part scientific exploration, the book details alternative strategies for preventing and treating cancer.

Dr. Servan-Schreiber was a thirty-one-year-old physician and neuroscience researcher at the University of Pittsburgh when he offered to serve as a healthy control in a brain scan experiment. To his and his colleagues' shock, the scan revealed a brain tumor. Surgery removed the tumor, but when he asked what he could do to prevent it from returning, the answer was, "Just go back to your normal life."

So he did, returning to a diet high in sugar and red meat with little to no exercise. The cancer returned aggressively. After enduring a second surgery, chemotherapy, and radiation, Dr. Servan-Schreiber turned to alternative medicine. He found mountains of research on the cancer-fighting properties of whole foods, herbs like turmeric and garlic, and the benefits of eliminating sugar, exercising, and practicing meditation.

He adopted a Siberian Husky puppy, whose boundless energy forced him into daily long-distance runs. In doing so, he tapped into the anticancer effects of oxygenation and intense exercise. He attributed his illness in part to pesticide exposure growing up in rural France and his poor diet and lifestyle.

Two discoveries frustrated him deeply: first, the existence of over one hundred thousand synthetic chemicals released into our environment since the Industrial Revolution; and second, that so many healing tools, including food, were ignored by conventional medicine.

Dr. Servan-Schreiber lived twenty more healthy years. With encouragement from his brother and colleagues, he compiled everything he'd learned into *Anticancer: A New Way of Life*. I've read it several times and developed an anticancer protocol for pets based on his findings.

This includes cruciferous vegetables, fish oils, mushroom extracts, and healing herbs.

I've given away dozens of copies of his book to families devastated by a cancer diagnosis, people who had never heard that food, fresh air, and exercise could play a role in healing. I scour used bookstores and library sales to keep copies on hand. It offers hope. And sometimes, that's the beginning of healing.

CHAPTER 33

ADDICTION AT BOTH ENDS OF THE LEASH

In order to address addiction, we must first understand the brain, specifically, which part we nourish and which part we sabotage. I call this the battle of the brains. At the root of much of our automatic behavior is the brainstem, or the Dinosaur Brain. This primitive part of the brain runs the basics—heartbeats, breathing, digestion, sensing danger—and it does so brilliantly, without conscious effort. It's what enables the fight-or-flight response and is shared with reptiles, birds, and mammals.

Layered just above it sits what I refer to as the Lizard Brain, known in neuroscience as the limbic system. This is the emotional center, governing hunger, pain, fear, pleasure, and impulse. As a veterinarian, I've worked with thousands of lizards, from geckos to iguanas to massive monitor lizards, and they don't wag their tails or show affection like dogs do. They couldn't care less about their offspring. Their lives are driven by survival, instant gratification, and instinct. The Lizard Brain operates on dopamine, the neurotransmitter of desire and reward. It tells us to repeat pleasurable behaviors, whether it's surfing, scrolling, sugar, or shopping.

When overstimulated, this part of the brain can spiral into anxiety, cravings, impulsivity, and addiction. Combine chronic stress, sleep deprivation, inflammatory processed foods, and sedentary lifestyles, and you get a society ruled by its Lizard Brain. It's the hijacking of our higher faculties. But we're not meant to live in survival mode. We are meant to evolve beyond it.

Above the Lizard Brain lies what I call the Dalai Lama Brain, known to neuroscientists as the prefrontal cortex. It's the home of reason, empathy, gratitude, and long-term decision-making. It's what allows us to weigh options, suppress impulses, and act with wisdom. In humans, this reflective, logical region makes up a full third of our neocortex. It's less developed in dogs, chimps, and completely absent in reptiles. Lizards have no interest in caring for their young. But in people like the Dalai Lama, this part of the brain is fully alive and harmonized with the lower centers. It's nourished by real food, rest, exercise, time in nature, and spiritual practice.

In 1978, I traveled to India and met the Dalai Lama in the mountain village of Dharamshala. He moved with grace and joy, surrounded by monks who revered him. Here was a living example of someone ruled not by impulse, but by contemplation and compassion. I realized the Dalai Lama Brain isn't reserved for monks. It's in all of us, waiting to be awakened.

Yet modern life does everything it can to sabotage it. Dopamine-fueled junk food, relentless media, overstimulation, and chronic stress feed the Lizard Brain and weaken the reflective strength of the prefrontal cortex. Cortisol rises. Gut inflammation increases. Serotonin plummets. And the cycle continues—more anxiety, more cravings, more disconnection.

Healing animals was straightforward. Healing people was infinitely more complex. Families would faithfully follow whole food diets for their pets, and watch them heal, while continuing to sabotage their own health with sugar, alcohol, and processed foods. Why? Because people are addicted. I dove deep into neuroscience and psychology to understand why smart people make self-destructive choices. The answer was both ancient and simple.

In every culture I visited, from Methodist and Catholic communities in California, to Jews in Israel, to Navajo healers, Aboriginal elders, Tibetan monks, Indian yogis, and African imams, I saw the same truth: *our physical condition reflects our spiritual condition.*

Addiction isn't just chemical. It's spiritual. And healing isn't just physical. It's a reawakening of purpose, presence, and connection.

Science is catching up to what Indigenous peoples have long known. The epigenome, the layer of environmental and emotional influence around our DNA, responds to nutrients, toxins, and even thoughts. Every thought, every bite, every belief is a message to our cells. Spiritual practice, kindness, and reverence for life literally change the chemistry of our bodies.

The most powerful medicine we have isn't in a prescription bottle. It's in the foods we eat, the thoughts we think, the time we spend in nature, and the belief that something greater than ourselves is at work. That's how we begin to shift from the Lizard Brain to the Dalai Lama Brain, and reclaim our health, our wholeness, and our humanity.

CHAPTER 34

MENTAL HEALTH AT BOTH ENDS OF THE LEASH

My family calls me "Mr. Happy." They claim I just go surfing every dawn and then play with puppies and kittens all day. I admit this isn't far from the truth. My daughters and wife also say I live in a happy bubble, far removed from the cares of the world. And I don't argue. Veterinary medicine has been a joyful and fulfilling career.

But there's a shadow side few people see, and even fewer believe.

It first revealed itself in my third year at UC Davis Veterinary School during Dr. Fowler's wildlife medicine and surgery course, a class I had been dreaming of. Among a small group of zoo-track students was Dr. William, a PhD student who had already earned his veterinary degree. He was sharp, quiet, composed, someone I admired. Six weeks into the course, Dr. Fowler entered class one morning, solemn and red-eyed. He shared the news: Dr. William had taken his life. The room fell silent. No one moved. It was the first time I glimpsed the unspoken despair that can hide behind a competent, composed exterior.

Later, I learned that Dr. William had used his knowledge and access to veterinary drugs to end his life. He had left notes, returned borrowed books, and made meticulous plans. People speculated a romantic heartbreak, but no one considered that it might have been the profession itself.

Years later, in 1991, I received a call from Dr. Peter Weinstein to attend an emergency meeting of local veterinarians. There had been five suicides in the Southern California area. All men, all practice owners. I was shocked. I loved my job. Veterinary medicine was, for me, The Greatest Job. But as Dr. Weinstein outlined their stories, a pattern emerged: the crushing weight of financial stress, emotional fatigue, and perfectionism. He introduced a new term, "compassion fatigue," which was the cost of caring too deeply for too long. Then he asked if anyone had ever considered suicide. One-third of the group raised their hands, and I was stunned.

The death of patients is a daily occurrence for veterinarians, especially in practices like ours that see a high percentage of birds and exotic animals. These species are experts at hiding illness until it's too late. By the time they show symptoms, they're often in critical condition. Some die in the middle of an exam or immediately after a surgery that seemed successful. The pressure to make the right call, to save the unsavable, to support grieving families. It's a relentless emotional toll.

My first euthanasia decision during my internship came without guidance. Doc Thorson, my mentor, was out of town. An elderly woman, Mrs. Doreen, brought in her sick cat Peaches. The diagnosis was end-stage kidney failure. When I suggested euthanasia, she gently refused, telling me that decision belonged to God. Instead, I made Peaches comfortable with fluids and vitamins. She returned days later, ready. I asked her what changed her mind since Peaches had improved. Her priest had told her it was an act of mercy and the right choice to alleviate suffering. As she held Peaches and said goodbye, I understood the sacred role we veterinarians play. We are not just healers, but navigators to the other side.

Over the years, I have written tens of thousands of condolence notes, as Doc taught me. It became a form of catharsis. Still, the weight of unexpected loss can be crushing. I remember losing Grace, a twelve-year-old German shepherd I spayed without complications. Hours later, she died. I surfed for two hours the next morning, rage and grief in every paddle. Then I called her family to say I was so sorry. No words could soften the blow.

Veterinary school selects for perfectionists, those willing to read textbooks by the inch and work without rest. Many of my classmates had never received less than an A grade or experienced the agony of defeat in sports. But perfection is a dangerous standard in medicine. Things go wrong, even for seasoned professionals. And when they do, the weight of failure can feel unbearable. Fortunately, I had already experienced and been humbled by many failures playing sports—missing free throws that would have won the game, striking out with the bases loaded, sitting on the bench in front of thousands. But nothing prepared me for losing a patient unexpectedly, and nothing ever hurt me as deeply.

Add to this the financial stress of practice ownership; long hours, mounting debt, and now, cyberbullying. Vets are publicly shamed by strangers online, often after doing their best in impossible situations. The suicide rate among veterinarians is three to four times higher than the national average.

Yet through all of this, I found ways to stay grounded. I was lucky. Nancy ran the business side of our practice. I could focus on medicine and my patients. I meditated, surfed, and found healing in nature. I discovered the power of the "Blue Mind"—the meditative and calming effects that come from being in or near the ocean—that helped me balance the darkness with light. And I found strength in community. After that 1991 meeting, local vets began gathering regularly for support. No one else in the Saddleback Valley has taken their life since.

Veterinary medicine exposes us to both ends of the emotional spectrum: puppy kisses one minute and euthanasia and tears the next minute. It requires courage, compassion, and connection. Without those, and without a support system, the weight can become too heavy. I've seen it happen. I've felt it start to happen. But with grace, gratitude, and a little help from the ocean, I've always found my way back to the light.

CHAPTER 35

GUT HEALTH AT BOTH ENDS OF THE LEASH

I was amazed by how much I learned about animal health while recently attending a conference on integrative human health care. While many of the attending doctors were studying animals to understand and treat human diseases, I was doing the reverse: learning about human health to help my animal patients and heal myself. Two foundational principles emerged in nearly every lecture. Food must *nourish* and *protect* both the liver and the microbiome. These were truths I had preached for decades in veterinary medicine. Drugs can treat symptoms, often with side effects, but only real food can prevent, treat, or even reverse the chronic diseases that have skyrocketed in recent decades.

The microbiome was the star of the show. I soaked in lecture after lecture on autoimmune diseases and gut health. Experiments I'd never heard of, because they were published in human medical journals, used animal microbiomes to demonstrate profound outcomes. In one study, gut bacteria from old, overweight rats were transplanted into young rats, who then aged and gained weight. But when the process was reversed, old rats regained youth and vitality. It was revolutionary, and humbling.

The trillions of microbes in the intestines of animals, and humans, play nearly identical roles. They are the quiet, unseen healers in our bodies. I realized I was no longer just feeding myself. I was feeding five pounds of vital bacteria who, in turn, fed and protected me. These "friendly flora" produce half the body's dopamine and 90 percent of its serotonin—the very chemicals that fuel joy, calm, and contentment. They are fundamental to mood, memory, immunity, and longevity.

I cringed at the realization of what my immune system and celiac disease had done to my gut lining. The autoimmune attack had stripped away my villi, microscopic fingers that absorb nutrients and protect the body from invaders. I had been destroying the very system that shaped my mood, focus, and resilience. And now I understand why untreated celiac disease often leads to dementia. The gut isn't just linked to the brain; it *is* a brain. A living, reactive, sensing organ deeply connected to the nervous, immune, and endocrine systems.

The gut, like a well-tended vegetable garden, flourishes with the right care: water, organic nutrients, and protection from toxins. But give it glyphosate (Roundup), gluten, sugar, and chronic stress, and it becomes a leaky pipe, where its "tight junctions" between epithelial cells open like broken bricks. Toxins seep into the bloodstream, and the immune system, overwhelmed, attacks anything in its path. For me, that meant my own tissues. Yet by simply eliminating gluten, my body healed. Within six months, a follow-up endoscopy revealed the lush return of thousands of villi.

No drugs, just food. *Real food.*

The parallels with animal medicine were uncanny. The same microbes protected parrots, poodles, and Persians. They provided 70 percent of immune function, blocked toxins from entering the bloodstream, metabolized short-chain fatty acids like butyrate (found in ghee), and repaired the mucous barrier of the colon. Most stunning of all was that they communicated directly with the brain, shaping mood, thought, and behavior.

I had already been trying to heal my microbiome since my celiac diagnosis. The human protocol mirrored my veterinary advice: Remove, Reinoculate, Repair. Remove toxic foods, reinoculate with probiotics, and repair the gut lining with vegetables, herbs, prebiotics, and nutrient-dense foods. Fortunately, there is an all-encompassing holistic veterinary supplement called Gussy's Gut that does all of that: reinoculates and repairs an animal's microbiome with fermented superfoods, prebiotics and postbiotics of the highest quality. I embraced garlic, onions, leeks, sauerkraut, asparagus, kombucha, and apple cider vinegar. I doubled down on intense exercise, surfing of course, as physical exertion had been shown to fuel both healthy microbial growth and brain fertilizer called Brain Derived Neurotrophic Factor. Stress, I learned, released cortisol, which demolished beneficial bacteria and allowed Gram-negative invaders to flourish. These pathogens devoured the protective mucous lining, the final layer shielding my bloodstream from chaos. It was a miracle I hadn't bled to death.

So I meditated more, a practice I learned at Santa Clara in 1973 for a required religious study course. I surfed more. I laughed more. I cared for my microbial allies like beloved pets.

Another fascinating tool was the fecal transplant, something veterinarians had practiced for years. For rabbits with often fatal diarrhea, we'd blend healthy poop into a slurry and pass it into the sick rabbit's stomach. Within hours, their stools would normalize. I recalled the famous UC Davis cow with a window in its side, used as a microbiome donor for other cattle. Dogs and cats now had access to encapsulated fecal transplants from AnimalBiome, a genius Bay Area company. Maybe someday, coffee shops will offer "crapuccinos," microbiome smoothies for your gut!

Veterinarians have known about "dysbiotic drift" for centuries, when chronic stress, poor diet, alcohol, and toxic processed foods kill off beneficial microbes and replace them with harmful ones. These invaders feast on the mucous lining, allowing poisons to leak into the bloodstream. I'll never forget a beloved bunny who died twelve hours after a routine spay. She had never been around dogs or cats and was so traumatized by the sounds of "predators" in the clinic that her gut flora flipped overnight. The surgery had gone perfectly. The stress killed her beneficial bacteria which then killed her. The UC Davis necropsy confirmed it. That loss still haunts me.

Three weeks after that human medicine conference, I attended a veterinary lecture on kidney disease. The speaker, both courageous and honest, told us the very prescription kibble she was required to recommend was worsening kidney function in pets by damaging their microbiome. She exposed what I had long suspected: dry food, no matter how "scientifically formulated," feeds dysbiotic drift. The preservatives harm gut flora, create toxins, and place additional burdens on the kidneys.

It was a daring message, one that risked backlash from pet food sponsors who fund veterinary schools. But she was right. I had seen it. The healing of both people and pets begins in the gut. The future of medicine for both human and veterinary is microbial.

And if we nourish our inner garden, it will, in turn, heal us.

CHAPTER 36

INFLAMMATION AT BOTH ENDS OF THE LEASH

The root causes of inflammatory illnesses are triggered by infections, stress, industrial food, and environmental toxins. These causes aren't limited to the ailments I personally faced, but extended to a spectrum of diseases including obesity, autism, Alzheimer's, depression, heart disease, diabetes, and cancer. As every healer knows, inflammation is a vital tool for healing acute injuries, and modern medicine excels at addressing those. But it struggles with chronic, smoldering inflammation, the kind that simmers silently for years and ignites the body from within.

I was reminded of the brilliance of the acute inflammatory response while treating Angus, a beloved pet rat who had stopped eating. Angus wasn't a rescued feeder rat, but one bred specifically for companionship. Despite his gentle background, Angus bit down hard when I palpated his abdomen and discovered a large, painful tumor. Blood gushed from my finger. My immune system responded exactly as it should, by mounting a rapid inflammatory response to kill off any harmful bacteria introduced by his teeth. My finger swelled, turned red, and sealed up with a fibrin clot. Two weeks later, all that remained was a faint scar. This was inflammation at its best—intense, localized, time-limited, and ultimately healing.

But modern life is not filled with such cleanly resolved injuries. We no longer flee lions or tigers. Instead, we battle traffic jams, tight work deadlines, college tuition bills, overbooked calendars, and overstimulated minds. Our bodies still pump out the same stress hormones, adrenaline, cortisol, and norepinephrine, but without the corresponding physical exertion that would normally burn them off. We stew in our stress chemistry, sedentary and stuck. The result? Fat accumulates around our midsections, in our organs, inside arteries and livers, becoming breeding grounds for chronic disease.

As of September 2024, the CDC reports that 40% of Americans are obese, 75% are overweight, 10% are severely obese, and 12% are diabetic. Even more alarming is that 25% of American children are obese and already battling the same inflammation-fueled chronic conditions as adults. This crisis traces back to the late 1970s, when highly processed factory foods and high fructose corn syrup were introduced en masse. With them came a rise in obesity, diabetes, and cancer—all stemming from uncontrolled, unresolved inflammation. I firmly believe that these manufactured foods are the primary culprits behind this epidemic, in both people and pets.

The danger of chronic inflammation is that it has a clear starting point, but no off switch. Unlike acute inflammation, which resolves after healing, chronic inflammation lingers and festers, eroding the body from the inside out. The specific diseases may differ, but the biochemical pathways and inflammatory markers look remarkably similar.

And so does the healing path:

Whole food, including mostly plant-based diets.

Outdoor movement.

Mindfulness and prayer.

Restorative sleep.

Intermittent fasting.

Anti-inflammatory supplements like ginger, turmeric, Ashwagandha, Boswellia, and vitamins C and D.

And joyful, social connection.

Western medicine excels at treating symptoms with pills and procedures. But integrative care seeks the root cause and addresses it with lifestyle and food. Always, *always* beginning with food.

The integrative doctors echo what I've witnessed in holistic veterinary medicine for years. They speak with conviction and present the evidence to support it, with peer-reviewed studies on the power of diet, movement, and meditation to reduce inflammation and reverse disease. Their message is clear: inflammation is not our enemy. It is a message. And we can answer it with nature, nourishment, and connection.

CHAPTER 37

AYURVEDA AT BOTH ENDS OF THE LEASH

In the decades following 2000, when life seemed steady and well, I got a wake-up call from an unlikely source, in an unlikely place.

Kelly had gone off to study abroad in tropical Queensland, Australia, with a group of Point Loma Nazarene University students drawn by the lure of warm waves and legendary surf. Australia had long been woven into our family's story. We had a revolving door of Aussie visitors, including former students, teammates, and colleagues. Their accents and laid-back humor brightened our days. In 2000, we took the girls to the Sunshine Coast, where Kelly competed in a surf contest and both she and Shawn fell in love with Australia's warmth, surf, and spirit. They soon signed up for a semester abroad.

When we flew over to visit, reconnecting with old friends and expat Americans, I discovered that my former yoga teacher from Melbourne, Shanti, had moved north too. She now ran a yoga and meditation institute in the tropics, and to my surprise, she was also a practicing Ayurvedic doctor. I had never heard of Ayurveda.

That was about to change.

Ayurveda, I learned, has been practiced continuously in India for over four thousand years. Its earliest practitioners also treated animals, making them, arguably, the first veterinarians. In fact, the first Ayurvedic veterinary hospital opened in 1463 BC, guided by a textbook written a millennium earlier. These early doctors could detect illness in a foal by palpating three different pulses on the mare's neck. I had no idea there was more than one pulse to feel.

The word *Ayurveda* comes from Sanskrit: *veda* means "knowledge," and *ayus* means "life." It is, simply, the science of life. Today, some of its best-known tools like turmeric, Boswellia, and ashwagandha are staples in both human and animal care at my practice. Ayurvedic medicine prevents and treats disease by nourishing the body through Sattvic diet (plant-based eating emphasizing clean, balanced, and seasonal food), herbs, movement with yoga asanas, meditation, and aligning with nature's rhythms.

We discovered that Shanti's wellness center was just a few miles from Kelly's university. We arrived jet-lagged yet thrilled to find Shanti unchanged and radiant as ever. She took one look at Nancy and me and said, with a smile, "Doug, Nancy—what has America done to you? You both look terrible." She meant it with love, but her words hit home.

She had long warned her yoga students that Americans were too distracted to hear the divine whisper within. "God has hidden himself inside all of us. But Americans are too busy to stop, look, and listen to God!"

She poured us steaming mugs of chai and added, "Too much work. Not enough meditation."

When I told her about my manic schedule, she invited me back for a full Ayurvedic evaluation. "Come for a week," she said. "Ayurveda will fix you."

Three months later, I returned.

After a harrowing rental car drive on the wrong side of the road, I reached Nirvana Wellness Sanctuary, seventy acres of dense subtropical forest in the Gold Coast hinterland. It was lush and remote, like Northern California with tree ferns. I was greeted by Shanti, her husband Peter, and two young assistants, Annie and Tonya, both on their way to becoming Ayurvedic doctors.

We gathered in the most pleasant "doctor's office" I'd ever seen: ginger tea, incense, and a view of the forest. Shanti asked about my daily habits. I described early-morning surfing; coffee and perhaps a quick bowl of granola, time-permitting; long workdays; skipped meals; late, slow dinners of healthy veggies and tofu; and very little sleep. Overall, I thought I was doing pretty well. Shanti disagreed.

"You call yourself a doctor and care for your body like a fool," she laughed. "Your body is exhausted. Your nails are cracked. Your lips are chapped, and your skin is dry. You are dehydrated, overworked, and out of balance."

I realized quickly that I was supposed to be drinking water.

The coffee and green tea weren't working as substitutes.

Annie and Tonya nodded as they examined my nails first. I had rows of parallel cracks running up and down on all my fingernails.

"You're lacking nutrients causing your nails to crack, like having a poor foundation for a house," Shanti said.

"Or you have a faulty digestive tract and you're not absorbing the nutrients to manufacture healthy nails."

I learned that Ayurvedic practitioners can diagnose imbalances just by reading signs from my external appearance, bypassing the high-tech diagnostics I was used to. According to their readings, I was prediabetic, had compromised kidneys, a weak heart, and my digestion was a mess.

"Am I dying?" I asked.

"Stick out your tongue so we can have a look," Shanti said.

All three looked long and hard at my tongue, from back to front, side to side, and under. They shared their notes again and Shanti nodded in agreement. She handed me a mirror and asked me to look at my tongue.

"See how the tip of your tongue deviates to the right, Doug? And do you see the deep furrow in your tongue and all the yellow discoloration? Now, look at Annie and Tonya's tongues."

The ladies giggled and then stuck out their tongues at me.

What a difference. Their tongues were uniformly bright pink, with no furrows or twists.

Shanti said, "All that yellow discoloration is toxins we call *ama*. In Ayurveda, the tongue is not just an origin of taste, but a tool for diagnosis and detoxification, and you're a mess, Doug! The front of your tongue is curved abnormally, which relates to the stomach, intestines, and heart. That deep furrow in your tongue is called *vata* imbalance. It represents your spine with evidence of injury, stress, insomnia, or bottled-up emotions. The yellow coating is a *pitta* imbalance and *pitta* toxins. Your tongue is also pale, indicating you have poor circulation, a low red cell count, and improperly digested foods. The good news is the back of your tongue, associated with the kidneys and large intestine, is not nearly as crooked as the front. Here's what you can do to get your tongue and digestive tract to start healing." They gave me a copper tongue scraper to remove the yellow coating of "ama," or undigested toxins.

Next the three women peered into my eyes to analyze my irises before examining my skin. They studied my face, back, chest, and feet. "You are so dry. You need to drink lots of water. How many kilos are you, Doug?" Shanti asked. I quickly did the math in my head, dividing 175 pounds by 2.2.

"Between seventy-five and eighty kilos," I answered.

"That's the minimum number of ounces you need to drink each day. And if you play basketball, you need to drink another twenty ounces at best," she replied.

Then they asked about my bathroom habits.

"How often do you pee, and what color is it?" inquired Annie.

"As little as possible and I don't look other than to make sure the toilet seat is up," I answered.

Shanti told me I needed to chart my urine color and how often. Dark yellow or water-like were two extremes to avoid.

"And now, Doug, what about your bowel movements? What is the shape, and does it float?" asked Tonya.

I thought they were joking, but they all had their pens poised to jot down my response. I talk and analyze animal and bird poop all day at work, but people poop is a taboo subject.

"Uh, gosh, I don't have a clue."

Shanti seriously told me that I needed to track my stools. She described perfect poop as being sigmoid-shaped, well-formed and floating, like a sea snake. She guaranteed that my poop would be transformed by the time my week was over.

I began to understand how the body gives us daily clues about our health, if we're willing to look.

I was told never to eat after 8:00 p.m. and to make lunch my biggest meal. They explained that eating late didn't allow the gastrointestinal track to rest, which was harmful. They also gave me water goals, sleep goals, and more yoga postures (asanas) to practice. I had assumed my joints were permanently stiff from sports injuries, but Shanti was confident Ayurveda could restore flexibility.

"Ayurveda will heal your arthritis. You'll sit in half lotus in three months," she said. "You just need sleep, water, and nourishment. Not coffee, Doug. Real nourishment."

My body resisted the yoga and meditation at first with my hips, knees, and ego aching, but something began to shift. I learned that Ayurveda is not just medicine. It's a way of life rooted in observation, simplicity, and deep connection with nature.

Meals at the retreat were vibrant and healing, sautéed vegetables in ghee, basmati rice, lentils, spices. Ghee, they explained, is rich in butyric acid, a critical fuel for gut health and cellular energy. A decade later, blood tests would confirm that I had low blood butyrate, which is an energetic food for the mitochondria in my intestinal cells. Healthy mitochondria, which serve as the cell's power source, are critical to health and cancer prevention. All of this was evidence that Shanti and her team had known more from an inspection of my body than Western doctors knew from brief exams and labs.

Years later an intestinal biopsy would confirm Shanti's diagnosis of my damaged digestive tract. I had celiac disease. My immune system was destroying the lining of my intestines, preventing me from absorbing vital nutrients and allowing toxins to leak into my body, causing severe joint pain. And all these maladies were cured by a gluten-free, natural diet like I advise all of my patients to eat.

Ayurveda reminded me what I had long believed as a veterinarian: that healing happens when we nourish the body, calm the mind, and support the spirit. It's the same for animals. They thrive on whole foods, fresh water, rest, and love. When we honor their nature, we also remember our own.

We are all meant to live in harmony—with ourselves, each other, and the planet. That's what Ayurveda taught me. Healing isn't found in pills. It's found in the rhythm of breath, in real food cooked with care, in stillness and movement, in scraping the tongue and watching the sunrise.

And just like the wisdom of animals, it's been here all along.

CHAPTER 38

QUANTUM SHAMANTICS AT BOTH ENDS OF THE LEASH

I finally made it to the annual meeting of the American Holistic Veterinary Medical Association. I'd been a member since 1988, ever since witnessing an astonishing hip dysplasia recovery through whole foods and supplements. I read their monthly journals cover to cover and embraced integrative care for all species. But I'd never made it to their annual meeting, typically held at the end of summer, the prime time for our family trips to Yosemite, Lake Tahoe, or warm-water surf spots with our extended clan.

Once the girls finished college and began their careers, I could finally attend. That year, the conference was conveniently held in San Diego. My name tag bore a little pink ribbon labeled "Newbie," branding me as a first-time attendee. It made me feel slightly sheepish, but it also filled me with anticipation. Four days of holistic veterinary talks awaited me, and all my holistic heroes were on the docket: Dr. Jean Dodds, Dr. Stephen Blake, Dr. Greg Ogilvie, and Dr. Cheryl Schwartz.

I spent mornings immersed in food therapy classes, afternoons learning from Dr. Dodds about autoimmune thyroid disorders and vaccinosis, or adverse reactions to vaccines. The next day, I heard Dr. Ogilvie speak on integrative cancer care. A former professor at Colorado State and author of the gold-standard veterinary oncology textbook, he spoke with clarity and conviction. He described a comprehensive approach to cancer, including whole foods, fish oil, and targeted supplements, all working in harmony with chemotherapy, radiation, and immunotherapy. He was lean, blond, and energized by both science and spirit. I learned he'd left academia for a specialty practice in San Diego and was also a triathlete. He understood the "Blue Mind" effect of the ocean. Since that day, I've referred countless cancer patients to his care.

Most days, I forgot to eat. Between lunchtime lectures and the exhibit hall, I was too engrossed. At the book display, I picked up Dr. Dodds's text on thyroid disease and another book that caught my eye: *Analog Medicine—A Science of Healing: Adopting the Logic of Quantum Mechanics as a Medical Strategy* by Dr. Ronald Hamm. The title alone intrigued me. Flipping through, I noticed a chapter on Jesus, the multitalented healer appearing in roles as ophthalmologist, audiologist, gynecologist, orthopedist, psychiatrist, and even one who could raise the dead. I bought it on the spot.

On the last day, the exhibit hall was closed, and I finally stopped for lunch. Still feeling self-conscious about my "Newbie" tag, I scanned the room for a quiet spot. That's when I noticed a lone cowboy, about my age, seated at an empty table. His dress code—well-worn Wranglers, plaid shirt, broken-in boots, and a black cowboy hat—made it easy to peg him as a large animal vet. I asked if I could join him. Instead of the expected grunt, he greeted me warmly and began peppering me with questions: "How long have you been a holistic vet? Where do you practice? What got you interested? What equipment do you use?"

Between bites of beetroot and quinoa salad, I answered them all. Finally, the cowboy spoke. "You know," he said, "it's not whether you have a twenty-thousand-dollar laser or a ten dollar one. You get the same effect if you believe it's going to heal and the patient believes you. Your intent, your mind, and the patient's mind—those are what control the healing. The instrument is just an intermediary."

I nearly spit out my salad. "Where do you practice?" I asked. "Not to be judgmental, but you look like a mixed animal vet who sounds like he's from Berkeley."

"Idaho," he replied with a grin. "I treat them all, but mostly cattle and horses. I gave up on the nonsense we learned in school. I'm interested in healing at the quantum level. Healing the whole animal, not prescribing a pill with ten side effects."

I told him he sounded like the author of the quantum healing book I'd just bought. He asked if I had it with me. I reached for it, and he turned it over to show me the back cover. "Would you like me to sign it?" he asked. I blinked. The cowboy was Dr. Ronald Hamm himself.

For the next hour, I bombarded him with questions. "It's God and the universe all working for good," he said. "We can help or harm, but it's our intent that shapes the outcome. Animals know. They can sense your beliefs. They choose to partner with you in healing, or they put up a wall if they doubt your sincerity."

I mentioned the chapter on Jesus. "After I started studying healing," he said, "I realized Jesus was describing a reality that modern science is only beginning to understand. It's quantum mechanics. What Jesus called love, maximizing vital energy through acceptance and nonjudgment, is what scientists now recognize as the Entanglement Principle. Energy invested in grudges or guilt is unavailable for healing. Heal yourself first. Then you can heal others."

They don't teach that in veterinary school. Or any school for that matter.

I've read Dr. Hamm's brilliant and unconventional book many times. I don't pretend to grasp the science, but I know indigenous healers have practiced this way for millennia. I call it *Quantum Shamantics*.

And I now follow Dr. Hamm's advice. I speak softly to every patient. I tell them what I'm doing and *why*: that we're here to help them feel better and return to their families. Instead of jabbing a needle into a coughing dog's vein to administer Lasix, I first explain the intent behind the medicine. I want the pet to know I'm here to heal, not harm.

Doc always told me, "You learn as much between the lectures as you do in class."

He was right. And sometimes, the biggest teachers wear boots and a black hat.

CHAPTER 39

HEALING BOTH ENDS OF THE LEASH

In a thrilling near-death experience, a young medical student and WWII soldier, George Ritchie, was declared dead from pneumonia and zipped into a body bag. But ten minutes later, he returned to life. In his book *Return from Tomorrow*, Dr. Ritchie recounts a profound journey, while he was declared dead, into another dimension where he encountered a "Being of Light" who radiated indescribable love. The experience forever changed him. He dedicated the rest of his life not to personal glory but to loving service.

Later, during the liberation of a Nazi concentration camp, Ritchie met a prisoner who radiated health and joy. Though imprisoned longer than most, he had chosen early on to love everyone he met—Jew or Nazi—and to forgive. "Love kept me alive," he explained. This echoes centenarian Dr. Gladys McGarey's wisdom that love is the best medicine. Yet none of us were taught this in veterinary or medical school.

As a veterinarian, I've witnessed the transformative power of love, particularly between pets and their people. Animals bring joy, companionship, and purpose. Walt Whitman called dogs "once-born souls," part angel, part canine. I agree. Though heartbreak is inevitable, the love they give us is worth every tear.

Across the globe, sages of every tradition teach the same thing. *We are here to love, to serve, and to forgive.* I've watched holy men and women in all corners of the world practice their faiths, from riverbanks in India to the cathedrals of Europe, from mosques in the Middle East to surfers greeting a sunset. And as Anne Frank believed, nature is the best place to remember that all is as it should be. This insight alone can shift our biology toward healing.

Science now affirms what the sages have always known: forgiveness, kindness, and gratitude change our epigenome, the switchboard that tells our genes how to express themselves. Toxic emotions, especially vindictiveness, damage that delicate wiring, whereas loving kindness can lead to resilience and vibrant health. The Holocaust survivor Ritchie met was glowing with life not because of nutrition or medicine, but because of his conscious choice to love and forgive. I have struggled to understand why people would refuse to forgive family, friends, and business partners who did them wrong. They would rather go to their graves than extend the white flag of peace.

I've also struggled to understand why people who watched their pets thrive on real food would refuse to make the same changes for themselves. Instead, they clung to pills and surgeries while continuing to consume the very foods making them sick. Their cravings, addictions, and inertia were stronger than logic.

That's when I realized: Willpower alone isn't enough. Spirit power is the missing piece.

The Lizard Brain craves sugar, impulsivity, and comfort. The Dalai Lama Brain, or our prefrontal cortex, longs for love, peace, and purpose. But the limbic system often hijacks our better judgment. Addictions are powerful and breaking the cycle takes more than science. It takes surrender.

For some, like me with celiac disease, willpower, pain, and fear of death triggered radical change. For others, only a higher power can shift the tide. Twelve-step programs are rooted in this truth. We are powerless on our own, but transformation begins when we surrender. Call it the Great Spirit, the Big Guy, Mother Nature, or God—when we ask for help, healing begins.

Spirit power can do what no pill can. It can shift the entire trajectory of our physiology, DNA expression, psychology, and purpose. It can silence addiction and amplify peace. It can heal the epigenome.

And it's free! No side effects, only miracles. I have met a dozen surfing pastors who in the blink of an eye went from murderous drug addicts to decades of ministry after surrendering their addictions to the Great Spirit and preaching Romans 8.

The night I finally began writing this book was moments after I ended Rudy's life.

I was alone at midnight with Rudy, our beloved Boston terrier, at our clinic. He had spent his last day in San Diego with Nancy and the girls enjoying their loving touch and a last seafood meal on San Diego Bay. I was stunned when we arrived at the clinic and Rudy walked into Luke's kennel, nuzzled up next to him, and shared a few bites of Luke's turkey dinner. Luke was the epileptic feline I twice rescued from euthanasia and had taken over Rudy's job as the clinic healer and comforter. Rudy hated Luke and was disgusted that an epileptic feline took his job when he moved to live with the girls. After his act of forgiveness, he walked over to where I was sitting on the floor and put his head on my lap and looked peacefully into my eyes as if he was ready for the journey of a lifetime.

With trembling hands and a broken heart, I put him to sleep and unleashed a monsoon of tears I didn't know existed in me. For hours, I sat on the clinic floor beside his still body, crying, writing, and releasing the grief I had carried for decades from euthanizing a thousand pets without shedding a tear. There was never a moment to mourn during our manic days at the clinic going from a euthanasia to greeting a new puppy in the span of three minutes. Rudy was our family's comic, our healer, our joyful companion. Despite a life filled with genetic defects, cancer since nine months, and autoimmune disease, he danced through life with panache.

His final illness, bladder cancer, was devastating. I tried everything I knew—whole foods, supplements, prayers, oncologists—but I could not heal him. That night, after helping him transition peacefully, the tears exploded, and I finally began to write. Rudy had taught me how to live with illness and, in the end, how to grieve. His forgiveness of Luke and of me was a reminder of the grace animals carry.

Five months later, we met Mugsy, a traumatized French bulldog. He had suddenly lost his elderly guardian and faced euthanasia after biting a paramedic who had tried to revive the deceased woman whom Mugsy was guarding.

At first, Mugsy was tense, broken, and reactive. But love, patience, and spirit power began to heal him.

Today, Mugsy is thriving, featured in *Forbes* magazine and known on Instagram as "Haze," the model for one of San Diego's craft beer labels. We like to think Rudy had a hand in sending him to us.

In closing, here is my final advice:

Get a pet. Love it. Feed it real food. Laugh with it. Mourn when it leaves.

Then go get another one.

Love and care for yourself the way you care for your pet. Eat real food. Move outside. Forgive. Ask for Spirit Power. Surrender what you can't control. Let nature, whole food, and kindness do the heavy lifting.

We are better people because of the animals in our lives. Better stewards of the earth. Better friends, family, and neighbors. Our health, and theirs, depends on the simple things, so it's time to get back to the basics. Real food, real love, and a reverence for the miracle of life.

Thank you, Rudy.

And thank you, dear reader, for healing both ends of the leash!

ACKNOWLEDGMENTS

Thank you to the many families of the Animal and Bird Clinic who suggested and inspired me to write and allowed me the honor and privilege to help care for their pets' health.

Thank you to the late Padre Don, whom I met at Santa Clara University—the finest field ecologist I have ever encountered, medical school dropout, book editor, and priest. Padre Don nagged me to finish the book and make it into two books. He read and edited the book multiple times in his late eighties. He also handed out the natural diet to many families in Northern California who then witnessed the magical healing powers of food.

Thank you to Rachel Lawrence, Catherine Harrison, and Cynthia Phillips who all turned my first six handwritten notebooks into a typed manuscript during their spare time.

Thank you to the multitalented, seventy-seven-year-old Marcia McCormack for offering to complete typing the other seven notebooks into a manuscript. She did this with alacrity, editing advice (make it two books), great humor, and kindness. She has been a trusted friend since the '90s, a published author, RN, energy healer, and knitting and ukulele maestro. This book would never have been completed without Marcia's great talent and time.

Thank you to the wonderful staff of healers at the Animal and Bird Clinic of Mission Viejo. I have never seen so much kindness, dedication, professionalism, and skill. It has been a humbling honor to work with our team of dedicated doctors for decades: Peter Bloch, Richard Mackey, Brett Hensley, Greg Myers, Leslie Hall, and Tina Stephens. Thank you to the talented, professional, and kind technicians Juan Infante and Rosa Flores who have awed me for two decades. Thank you to Sarah Sturtevant, Mike Walling, Amy Joyce, and Matthew Marks who all managed the business office for many years. Thank you to our twenty-four staff members who went to veterinary school and are now healers all over the country. And thank you to our beloved front reception staff who have the most demanding job and are the face of the practice to the public: You Are The Best!

Thank you to my friends and neighbors Dibi and Herbie Fletcher—both artists, writers, and surfers who gave me the best advice ("Keep it simple, dude!") and introduced me to their friends, Bill and Gayle Gladstone of Waterside Publishing. To my surprise, they all encouraged me to publish these stories and make two books, one of which is the memoir coming next!

Also, thank you to Dibi and Gayle for recommending Lilly Barels to be the final editor when I could not figure out how to turn 594 typed pages of scientific rambling into a pleasant read. Lilly took her UCLA neuroscience and world dance degree for a journey to the North Shore of Oahu instead of medical school as planned. She is an editor, author, yoga and healing arts instructor, art and science teacher, wife, and mom! Lilly was the perfect editor to combine the science with the soul of the stories. A big *mahalo* to Lilly!

Many thanks to daughters Kelly and Shawn who were tiny tots in July 1991 when we took over the Animal and Bird Clinic. You have been my greatest joy in life and were always supportive of the endless late-night and weekend emergencies. You encouraged this book from the moment I brought up the idea. Like your mother, you are world-class adventurers and travelers who found great joy seeing wildlife in wild places.

Last, and most important, thank you Nancy, for being there every step of the accidental journey into veterinary medicine, starting with Sam the sugar glider in Melbourne. You have faithfully and lovingly supported all my clumsy efforts along the way, many of which ended in disaster! Without you, neither the Animal and Bird Clinic nor this book would have been possible. Thank you, thank you, thank you for doing an impeccable job running the business as the original remote worker so you could always be at home for the girls, and I could focus entirely on healing. Thank you for fulfilling your dream to build the most beautiful vet hospital that brought the outside world in! Nancy: I look forward to more adventures with you—the greatest traveler to wild places I have ever known! I love you.

TCVM Food Therapy Chart

(Traditional Chinese Veterinary Medicine)

Pet name: _____

Primary Complaints: _____

Uses/ Indications	Meat & Dairy (Dogs 60%, Cats 80%)	Vegetables & Fruits (Dogs 30-40%, Cats 10-20%)	Grains/Beans/Other (Dogs and Cats 0-10%)
Inflammatory (Seniors with arthritis)	Chicken, Chicken liver, Goat milk, Ham, Lamb kidney and liver, Lobster, Mutton, Pheasant, Prawn, Shrimp, Venison	Apricot, Blackberry, Cherry, Citrus, Coconut, Ginger, Garlic, Papaya, Peach, Pepper, Plum, Pumpkin, Quinoa, Raspberry, Tangerine, Turmeric	Brown sugar, Malt sugar, Oats, Olive oil, Rice vinegar, Sorghum, White rice
Anti-inflammatory (Allergies, Vomiting, Diarrhea, Arthritis, Cancer, Seizures)	Cod, Crab, Duck, Duck egg, Egg white, Herring, Mussel, Oyster, Rabbit, Scallop, Shark, Turkey, White fish, Yogurt	Alfalfa, Apple, Banana, Blueberry, Broccoli, Celery, Cucumber, Eggplant, Gingko, Kelp/Seaweed, Kiwi, Mango, Mushroom, Orange, Pear, Persimmon, Spinach, Strawberry, Tomato, Watermelon	Barley, Barley sprouts (green), Brown rice, Flax seed oil, Green tea, Honey, Sesame oil, Tofu
Neutral (Healthy cats and dogs)	Beef, Beef liver, Bison, Chicken eggs, Mackerel, Milk (Cow's), Pork, Pork kidney and liver, Quail, Salmon, Sardines, Tripe, Trout, Tuna	Cabbage, Carrots, Cauliflower, Ginkgo, Lemon, Pineapple, Sweet potato, Shiitake mushroom, Yam	Black bean, Green beans, Green peas, Kidney beans, Red beans, Soybeans
Increasing Energy (Low Thyroid)	Beef, Chicken, Herring, Mackerel, Rabbit, Rumen (cow, goat), Trout	Pumpkin, Shiitake mushroom, Squash, Sweet potato, Yam	Oats
Blood Repair (Anemia, Liver disease)	Beef, Eggs, Heart, Liver, Sardines	Apricots, Carrots, Dates, Parsley	Kidney beans
Diabetes, Cushing's Disease	Duck, Eggs, Goat milk, Pork, Rabbit, Turkey	Apples, Asparagus, Lemon, Mango, Pears, Spinach, Tomatoes	Black beans, Honey, Kidney beans, String beans, Peas, Tofu
Anti-cancer	Chicken (organic), Lamb (organic), Turkey (organic)	Apple, Broccoli, Carrot, Garlic, Ginger, Citrus peel, Kale, Mushrooms, Mustard greens, Orange, Parsley, Pear, Radish, Seaweed, Spinach, Turmeric	Apple cider vinegar, Green tea, Honey, Peppermint

Feed **1 cup per 10 pounds body weight per day** unless otherwise directed (total may be split between meals)

☐ Raw (Fruits, Carrots, Dairy)

☐ Lightly cooked (Meat, Fish, Vegetables, Mushrooms, Grains)

☐ Supplements (Missing Link, Fish oils)

Clinician: _____   Date: _____

WELLNESS CHECKLIST FOR PETS

- Daily exercise for 40 minutes minimum to achieve a lean, muscular body. Animal studies found this increases longevity by 33% and decreases chronic disease by 50%
- High-quality/home-prepared whole food diet with whole food supplements, i.e., Missing Link/Standard Process, Welactin fish oils, and Gussy's Gut for microbiome health
- Annual comprehensive exam
- Yearly grading of teeth (1–4) plus regular dental cleaning and daily brushing of teeth, if possible
- Yearly wellness blood tests, twice yearly for Super Seniors (12 years and older)
- Year-round internal and external parasite control: many herbal and medicinal products
- Yearly vaccine evaluation for lifestyle. Vaccine titers after initial puppy/kitten vaccines
- Yearly internal fecal parasite exams and blood parasite tests: heartworm, tick bite diseases (ehrlichiosis, Lyme disease, Rocky Mountain spotted fever, anaplasmosis)

"Health is the presence of a superior state of well-being—a vigor, a vitality, that has to be worked for day after day."

> —Dorian "Doc" Paskowitz, MD (1921–2014),
> Stanford University, Physician/Surfer

"The Billion Dollar Pills"

If the pharmaceutical industry could bottle the positive medical benefits of these practices, they would be Billion Dollar Pills. They are essentially free and available to all:

General Health Checklist

- Fun daily, early-morning, outdoor exercise in or near water, like swimming, surfing, dog walking, or jogging, to achieve lean body mass, which increases longevity by 33% and decreases chronic disease in animal studies by 50%
- Whole food diet with no processed food. Mostly a variety of colorful plants and a palm-size serving of wild-caught fish or grass-fed animals that nourish the microbiome and liver. For those of us with autoimmune disease (fifty million Americans), eliminate gluten (wheat, oats, barley rye), sugar, grains, dairy, and the nightshade family
- Warm/hot yoga: pranayama breathing exercises and asana stretching exercises to increase strength, flexibility, balance, detoxification, cardiovascular health, stress reduction and weight management
- Meditation/prayer: 30–60 minutes daily to increase cardiovascular health, boost immune function, reduce stress, improve sleep, improve memory, increase kindness, and control pain. For students, it will increase your GPA and performance in sports. I started with Transcendental Meditation for a college class in 1973 for those two reasons and have added additional practices/prayers over the years

- Restful sleep (7–8 hours for adults and 8–10 hours for teenagers): read Dr. Matthew Walker's brilliant book, *Why We Sleep.* I foolishly damaged my health with sleep deprivation as a teenager until my mid-sixties. Sleep promotes growth and repair, cardiovascular health, immune support, memory and learning, brain detoxification, and improved sports performance in athletes, especially basketball players. Lack of sleep increases cardiovascular disease, cancer, stroke, diabetes, anxiety, weight gain and decreases academic success, sports performance, and medical decision-making for sleep-deprived doctors

Medical Checklist for Wellness and Autoimmune Care

- Regular dental cleaning: periodontal disease triggers autoimmune disease, cardiovascular disease, and kidney disease
- Parasite control: internal parasites and external tick bites and mosquito bites cause a multitude of disease symptoms and trigger autoimmune disease. More than sixty million Americans are infected, undiagnosed, and untreated according to the CDC. Many different tests and treatments are available. Check with your integrative doctor for testing and treatment
- Annual blood tests and physical exam with an integrative/functional medicine doctor
- Microbiome evaluation every few years, including fecal tests to ensure you have the right ratio of healthy, beneficial microbes in the intestines